THE
INFLUENTIAL
LEADER
BLUEPRINT

ACTION-ORIENTED
STRATEGIES TO ENHANCE
— YOUR —
LEADERSHIP CAPABILITIES
& DRIVE YOUR TEAM TO
PEAK PERFORMANCE

DR. RHONDA L. ANDERSON

THE INFLUENTIAL LEADER BLUEPRINT

Action-Oriented Strategies to Enhance Your Leadership Capabilities & Drive Your Team to Peak Performance

THE INFLUENTIAL LEADER
BLUEPRINT POWER MOVE TOOLS

Visit www.beinfluentialnow.com

Download free resources to enhance your leadership capabilities, drive your team(s) to peak performance, and achieve exceptional outcomes.

The password is: BINow2025 (Case Sensitive)

DEDICATION

To my husband, James Anderson, the love of my life—thank you for being my anchor, my confidant, and my unwavering supporter. Your belief in me has been the wind beneath my wings, giving me the courage to soar to new heights.

To my three amazing sons, Corwin, James II, and Elijah—you are my greatest joys and proudest accomplishments. Watching each of you grow into strong, compassionate, and driven men has been the honor of a lifetime. Your love, laughter, and encouragement fuel my passion and remind me every day of the importance of legacy and leadership.

To my beloved mother, Rosa L. Davis—though you are no longer here, not a day goes by that I don't miss you. I am forever grateful for the love, wisdom, and strength you instilled in me, and I am blessed to have had you as my mother.

With all my love...XOXO

TABLE OF CONTENTS

INTRODUCTION

Welcome to *The Influential Leader Blueprint: Action-Oriented Strategies to Enhance Your Leadership Capabilities & Drive Your Team to Peak Performance*! First, I want to personally thank you for purchasing my book. I am honored and I appreciate you! It is my hope that by the time you finish reading this book, you will be empowered to lead with greater impact personally and professionally. Lastly, that you are equipped with the knowledge and tools to gain greater influence within your organization, your team, and with external stakeholders you are connected to.

Some people may read this book because they have a genuine interest in leadership development and may not have a desire to lead teams. On the other hand, you are reading this book for one of two reasons:

1. You are an experienced leader who lacks one or more leadership capabilities, you are struggling to lead your team effectively, and you are looking for strategies to take your leadership to the next level.

2. You are an emerging leader who has a desire to lead a team in the future or you have just started leading a team and you are finding it difficult to gain respect as a leader, manage productivity, and/or struggle with team dynamics.

Basically, you are a person who wants to elevate your leadership game and you are seeking practical approaches that will support you on your professional journey!

I know, leadership is not for the faint at heart. In this high-pressure professional landscape, you are expected to excel in so many areas of leadership and may not have had the training and development needed to do so. You are overwhelmed with balancing operational demands and still have to make time to think and plan strategically. Developing and retaining talent is an ongoing concern of yours and an issue that your organization is wrestling with. Our economy is in a state of uncertainty and navigating organizational change is a challenge.

In addition, you are expected to be more "people focused" and fostering a culture of innovation and adaptability for your team is at the forefront. At this very moment, our workforce is very diverse and consists of people from different cultures and teams are multigenerational. This is another challenge you are facing as a leader. Lastly, managing remote, hybrid, and onsite employees is also a challenge you may be facing and when you don't have formal policies in place, this adds flames to the fire.

I could go on and on about your struggles as a leader, but let's focus on turning things around for the better. You can have it all as a leader and be influential! It starts with you being open to change and being intentional with execution. Becoming an influential leader takes work and you must shift your mindset to make it happen. I wrote this book as a blueprint to show that you can become the leader you want to be and are expected to be. I truly believe that you start with the end in mind. This will require you to envision yourself as the influential leader you are called to be. Take advantage of every opportunity where you can show up as the leader you are striving to be. This will accelerate your progress towards becoming influential.

Now, allow me to introduce myself...I am Dr. Rhonda Anderson! I have a Ph.D. from Mercer University, GO BEARS! I have 15+ years of experience in the talent development space in different capacities. I have worked in higher education, corporate, and in the non-profit arena. In addition, I am a certified professional coach with 10+ years of experience coaching leaders at every level. I am now the author of three books and I have a personal goal to author two more books in my lifetime. I can't say that I am a best seller, that was never my goal. I do know that my books have impacted thousands of people in a positive manner. This was always my goal!

After being laid off from my job, I launched "Silver Hawk Coaching & Consulting". Silver Hawk Coaching & Consulting specializes in providing comprehensive talent development services tailored to small and midsized organizations. Our expert team focuses on enhancing employee skills, fostering leadership, and driving organizational growth through customized coaching and consulting solutions. We understand the unique challenges these businesses face and offer personalized strategies to unlock their full potential. By investing in talent development, our team will help your organization build stronger teams, improve performance, and achieve long-term success. Organizations partner with us to empower their workforces and transform their businesses.

I know my bio sounds like I have always had it altogether! I want you to know that I have been a leader struggling to be influential and high performing. Most of my career, I didn't even see myself as a leader and thought that being a leader was associated with a title. For many years, I worked in toxic environments and was looked over for promotions. I found myself in a management role and had not had any formal training on how to be a manager and a leader. I was overwhelmed with the demands of my team. The lack of respect from my team was depressing, and I knew that I was missing some of the qualities a successful leader needs. Fear had me paralyzed and I was not confident in myself nor my performance.

I went into a mode of taking control of my leadership development journey. I read tons of books, attended training, and binge watched videos. This was draining and challenging because there was no one resource where I could get great action-oriented strategies from. I had a candid heart to heart conversation with my manager and she started giving me experiences that built my confidence and showed she trusted me. I could finally see the light, my influence increased, the overall performance of my department increased, and my relationships with my team members as a group and individually were enhanced as well. That position was the starting point of me experiencing many years of success as a leader! I am thankful that I have been able to develop and mentor other leaders to be the very best version of themselves. All of the strategies in this book are the same strategies I have applied when leading and managing a team or training and coaching other leaders. I attribute all of my successes in my career as a leader to remaining open to listening, being a continuous learner, and being coachable.

The purpose of *The Influential Leader Blueprint: Action-Oriented Strategies to Enhance Your Leadership Capabilities & Drive Your Team to Peak Performance* is for emerging and experienced leaders to have access to a guide that will equip them with innovative strategies to be the best leader possible, while managing their team(s) effectively. This book is not theory based; it is practical! My goal was to produce a leadership development book that you could pull off of your book shelf or out of your desk drawer at any time to reference when handling real world situations.

#BeInfluential

Remember, being a leader does not have to be complicated. It is all about being willing to take imperfect action and being intentional about wanting to be a better leader for yourself and your sphere of influence. When you start thinking that you know everything, that's when the learning stops and you become stagnant. It will definitely show in your performance. Take time to really evaluate where you are and commit to becoming better. Reading this book is one thing, but again, what will you do to implement and execute on the strategies shared. When I talk with leaders, many of them say I have already heard this or that. My question is, what have you executed and/or implemented? Let's start getting comfortable with taking action.

It is time to be influential!

Dr. Rhonda L. Anderson

CHAPTER

01

SOARING WITH PURPOSE: UNLOCKING THE POTENTIAL OF TRANSFORMATIVE LEADERSHIP

> "
>
> Leaders must learn how to effectively balance the management of people and organizational priorities. They are both equally important."
>
> **DR. RHONDA L. ANDERSON**
>
> "

A Journey from Manager to Leader

I vividly recall the day I was promoted to management. It was exhilarating, a moment of validation for my hard work, dedication, and potential. The rush of excitement fueled me in those early days; I was eager to make a difference and prove my worth.

But as weeks turned into months, the initial thrill began to fade. My days became consumed by meetings, deadlines, and an unending stream of emails. The excitement of my new role quickly transformed into a relentless juggling act. I was balancing organizational demands with the needs of my team. I found myself drowning in the pressure, constantly reacting instead of leading with intention, trying to keep up with the relentless pace.

Then came a pivotal moment. After a particularly difficult meeting, I had an epiphany: my struggles weren't just a result of a heavy workload. They were a symptom of a deeper issue. I had been thrust into a leadership role without any formal training. As an individual contributor, I had excelled at my tasks, but managing people required an entirely different skill set. I realized I wasn't truly leading; I was simply managing by default, reacting to problems instead of proactively guiding my team.

I knew something had to change. I refused to become another overwhelmed manager, merely going through the motions, burning out, or failing to inspire. I wanted to lead with impact.

Determined to grow, I committed to becoming a better leader. I actively sought out mentors, attended leadership training sessions, devoured every book I could find on the subject, and most importantly implemented what I learned. Every day, I asked myself, *how can I improve? What skills do I need to develop? What am I missing?*

It became clear that leadership wasn't just about acquiring knowledge; it was about applying it, refining my approach, and committing to continuous growth. The journey of self-awareness and intentional development transformed not just me but my entire team.

Today, I continue to walk this path because I believe leadership isn't a destination. It's a daily commitment to being the best version of yourself, for both your team and the mission you serve.

What Is Effective Leadership, and Why Does It Matter?

Effective leadership is more than just managing tasks or issuing directives. It's the art of inspiring others, making tough decisions with integrity, and creating a compelling vision that motivates people to take action. True leadership is rooted in influence, empathy, resilience, and the ability to connect on a human level. It's the ability to guide individuals and teams toward a common goal while fostering a culture of trust, respect, and innovation.

The impact of effective leadership extends far beyond an individual team or organization. Leaders shape cultures, drive innovation, and influence the lives of those they lead. They are the catalysts for change, helping teams navigate challenges, adapt to new circumstances, and embrace new opportunities. Strong leadership leads to engaged employees, higher productivity, and long-term success for the organization. Conversely, ineffective leadership can result in high turnover, low morale, and stagnation. The ripple effects of leadership, whether positive or negative, are profound, making it a critical factor in any organization's success. You must cultivate self-awareness, embrace continuous learning, and commit to leading with both purpose and authenticity.

Are you ready to step into that version of yourself?

The Biggest Challenges Leaders Face Today

Today's leaders are navigating one of the most complex and fast-paced environments in history. Rapid technological advancements, economic uncertainties, shifting workforce expectations, and global instability have transformed the leadership landscape. Navigating these challenges requires adaptability, resilience, and continuous growth like never before. Understanding these hurdles is the first step toward overcoming them.

1. **Navigating Rapid Change:** The speed of change in today's business world is unprecedented. From sudden market shifts to regulatory updates, leaders must pivot quickly and guide teams through uncertainty. The ability to anticipate trends, embrace agility, and communicate change effectively separates great leadership from those who struggle to keep up. This requires not only strategic foresight but also the ability to pivot and guide teams through uncertainty.

2. **Technological Disruption & AI:** The rise of artificial intelligence, automation, and digital transformation present both opportunities and challenges. While these innovations can streamline operations and improve efficiency, they also disrupt industries and redefine job roles. Leaders must leverage new technologies to remain competitive while managing the implications for their workforce. Balancing innovation while maintaining a human touch is essential.

3. **Economic & Geopolitical Volatility:** Global instability, economic downturns, and geopolitical tensions create volatile business conditions. Leaders are often required to make high-stakes decisions with limited information and intense pressure. The ability to stay agile, manage risk, and maintain a clear vision during uncertainty is essential.

4. **Multi-Generational Leadership:** Today's workforce spans multiple generations, each with unique values, communication styles, and expectations. Leading a diverse, multi-generational team requires emotional intelligence, flexibility, and a commitment to fostering an inclusive, collaborative environment.

Are You Ready to Lead Under Pressure?

The reality is these challenges aren't going away. The modern business environment will continue evolving at a relentless pace. If you are not prepared to lead under pressure, embrace change, and make strategic decisions, or navigate challenges, then leadership may not be for you. Leaders have to be intentional about staying ahead of these challenges, make the best strategic decisions, and keep in mind how these challenges will impact their organizations, internal stakeholders, and external stakeholders.

The 5 Essential Leadership Characteristics You Must Master

While many traits contribute to great leadership, there are five non-negotiable characteristics that **every** leader must master to be highly effective in today's fast-evolving world. Leadership is not for the faint of heart—your goal is to shift from merely surviving to thriving. These core traits will not only elevate your leadership abilities but also set you apart as a transformational force within your organization.

1. **Emotional Intelligence (EQ): The Foundation of Leadership**

   Emotional intelligence is the cornerstone of exceptional leadership. It involves self-awareness, emotional regulation, empathy, and strong interpersonal skills. Leaders with high EQ:

   ✦⁺ Build trust and credibility within their teams.

   ✦⁺ Navigate conflict with tact and diplomacy.

   ✦⁺ Create a work environment where employees feel valued and understood.

   Without emotional intelligence, even the most strategic leader will struggle to connect, influence, and inspire.

2. **Adaptability: Thriving in Uncertainty**

   Change is the only constant, and leaders who can adapt quickly to new situations are more successful. Adaptability is not only about being open to new ideas, learning from setbacks, and adjusting your approach as needed. It's not about having all the answers but being willing to find them.

Great leaders don't have all the answers. Instead, they:

✦ Stay open to new ideas and perspectives.

✦ Learn from both successes and failures.

✦ Pivot when necessary to keep the organization moving forward.

In a world of constant disruption, rigid leaders get left behind.

3. Visionary Thinking: Seeing Beyond the Present

Effective leaders have a clear vision for the future and can communicate it in a way that resonates with their team. Visionary leaders inspire action by setting a compelling direction and aligning their team's efforts toward a shared goal. They see beyond the immediate and make decisions that propel the organization forward.

Visionary Leaders:

✦ Set a compelling direction that energizes their team

✦ Align daily actions with long-term strategic goals

✦ Make decisions that position the organization for sustainable success

Having a vision isn't enough. Leaders must communicate clearly and consistently so that others can rally behind it.

4. Accountability: Leaders who hold themselves and their teams accountable create a culture of responsibility and excellence. Accountability means setting clear expectations, providing constructive feedback, and taking ownership of both successes and failures. When leaders model accountability, they foster trust, encourage continuous improvement, and reinforce a standard of excellence that keeps everyone committed to achieving their best.

Accountable Leaders:

✦ Set clear goals and expectations

✦ Provide constructive feedback that fosters growth

✦ Own both successes and failure

5. **Communication Skills:** Communication is the lifeblood of leadership. Effective leaders articulate their vision clearly, listen actively, and foster an environment where open dialogue thrives. Strong communication minimizes misunderstandings, strengthens relationships, and ensures alignment across teams and organizations.

Don't get me wrong, all the leadership characteristics you have read and heard about are important. However, the traits listed above help you establish a solid foundation for effective leadership.

By dedicating more time to developing this foundation, you will be better equipped to lead people through difficult times with clarity. More often than not, you will not fold under pressure, giving your team the security they need in your leadership.

Effective Leaders:

- ✦⁺ Set a compelling direction that energizes their team
- ✦⁺ Align daily actions with long-term strategic goals

Understanding Your Leadership Style: When to Adjust or Change It

Every leader has a distinct style shaped by their personality, experiences, and beliefs. However, effective leaders recognize that no single style works in every situation.

Being rigid in your leadership approach can limit your effectiveness—especially when leading diverse teams or navigating complex challenges. Understanding your dominant leadership style is essential, but knowing when to adjust it is what separates good leaders from great ones.

Six Common Leadership Styles

There are many different leadership styles, but here are the six most commonly recognized ones:

- ✦ **Autocratic:** Centralized decision-making approach with little input from others. Best used in high-pressure situations where quick, decisive action is required.

- ✦ **Democratic:** Encourages team involvement in decision-making, fostering engagement and buy-in. This approach is highly effective in collaborative environments.

- ✦ **Laissez-faire:** A hands-off approach that allows team members to take the lead. Works well with highly skilled and self-motivated teams but requires trust and accountability.

- ✦ **Transformational:** Focuses on inspiring and motivating teams by emphasizing vision, innovation, and change. Ideal for driving transformation within an organization.

- ✦ **Transactional:** Relies on structure, rules, and rewards/punishments to manage performance. This style is effective in maintaining consistency and meeting established goals.

- ✦ **Coaching:** Focuses on collaboration, support, and guiding team members toward growth and professional development by nurturing their individual strengths. These leaders are visionaries who inspire their teams to embrace each other's unique skills while motivating them to passionately commit to a shared goal.

Understanding your leadership style is the first step; the next is recognizing when to adjust your approach based on the needs of your team and the situation. Effective leaders are not confined to a single style; they are versatile and adaptive, continually refining their approach to fit the context.

How to Adapt Your Leadership Style to Situations & Team Dynamics

Throughout my journey as a leader, I have never been able to rely on one leadership style to solve every challenge when leading a team. If you have successfully led using only one type of leadership style—first, kudos to you. Second, that is not a sustainable or healthy way to lead. I have had to adapt my style based on the situation, and that ability to pivot has been critical to my growth as a leader. Adjusting your leadership approach is a vital skill that can make or break your effectiveness. Here are key strategies to help you refine your leadership style based on different situations and team dynamics:

- **Start by Evaluating the Situation.** Take a moment to assess the context you're working in. If your team is facing a tight deadline, a more direct approach may be necessary to keep things on track. However, if it's a creative project, encouraging collaboration and open dialogue will likely yield better results. Understanding the circumstances will guide you in choosing the most effective leadership style.

- **Consider your team members.** Every individual brings unique strengths, weaknesses, and motivations to the table. Some team members thrive on detailed guidance, while others prefer autonomy. By tailoring your approach to fit the specific needs of each person, you can optimize both their performance and overall team cohesion.

Stay flexible and be ready to pivot. What worked for your team yesterday may not be what they need today. If you notice that your initial leadership strategy isn't producing the desired results, don't hesitate to adjust your approach. Being adaptable shows that you are responsive to the evolving needs of both your team and the project.

Communicate your approach clearly. When you adjust your leadership style, explain why you're doing so. Transparency builds trust and helps your team understand the rationale behind your decisions. This alignment ensures that everyone remains engaged and committed to the team's goals.

Balancing Authority and Collaboration

The balance between authority and collaboration is delicate but crucial. Leaders must know when to take charge and when to empower their teams. Too much authority can stifle creativity, while too much collaboration can lead to indecisiveness.

Striking this balance requires a strategic approach:

- Set Clear Expectations- Define when decisions will be made individually and when they will involve group input to prevent confusion and empower the team.

- Foster Inclusivity- Encourage team members to voice their ideas to create a collaborative environment that promotes innovation and engagement.

- Be Decisive When Needed- Some moments call for firm leadership. Leaders should confidently take the lead when necessary, ensuring that decisions are well-informed and communicated effectively.

- Encourage Shared Leadership- Empowering team members to take ownership of their work not only distributes responsibility but also strengthens team cohesion and accountability.

Eight Strategies to Help You Level-Up Your Leadership

In today's rapidly evolving workplace, relying on traditional management tactics is no longer enough—it's time to level up. With shifting workforce expectations, the rise of remote and hybrid teams, and a growing emphasis on diversity and inclusion, leaders must embrace a more dynamic and emotionally intelligent approach.

Now more than ever, effective leadership requires a blend of strategic vision, adaptability, and the aptitude to cultivate an environment of trust and psychological safety. Here are eight strategies to help you level-up your leadership:

1. **Prioritize People Over Processes:** Building strong relationships and supporting your team's development should be a top priority. People are your most valuable asset. When you invest in their growth and well-being, you cultivate a more engaged and productive team.

2. **Execute with Conviction:** Great leaders make decisive, well-informed choices and take action with confidence. Trust your instincts, support your decisions with sound reasoning, and remain adaptable as new information emerges.

3. **Practice Active Listening:** Effective communication starts with listening. Give your full attention to your team members, validate their perspectives, and incorporate their feedback to inform your decisions. Active listening shows respect and builds trust.

4. **Create a Feedback-Rich Environment:** Feedback should be a two-way street. Cultivate a culture where constructive feedback is encouraged, received openly, and acted upon. This openness drives continuous improvement and strengthens your team's performance.

5. **Cultivate Resilience:** Challenges are inevitable, but resilient leaders bounce back stronger. Leading with resilience helps you navigate uncertainty and inspire your team to do the same.

6. **Invest in Your Development:** Leadership is an ongoing journey. Commit to continuous learning through reading, attending workshops, coaching, and seeking out mentorship. The more you invest in your own growth, the more effective you will be as a leader.

7. **Model the Behavior You Want to See:** Lead by example. Demonstrate the values, work ethic, and professionalism you expect from your team. Your actions set the standard and shapes your workplace culture.

8. **Foster Psychological Safety:** Create an environment where your team feels safe to express ideas, ask questions, and take risks. Psychological safety enhances creativity, problem-solving, and team cohesion.

Leaders who sharpen their emotional intelligence, foster collaboration, and promote resilience are better equipped to navigate complexity and drive innovation. Elevating leadership skills is not just about staying relevant, it's about empowering teams to thrive and sustain high performance in an ever-changing landscape.

Dr. Rhonda's Leadership Lessons: A Continuous Journey of Growth

Remember, accepting a leadership role is a commitment to continuous improvement. Leadership is not a static position, it's a dynamic journey that requires ongoing reflection, learning, and adaptation. The best leaders are those who remain curious, embrace change, and commit to becoming better every day.

When you lead with purpose, prioritize people, and invest in your growth, you'll not only elevate your leadership effectiveness but also inspire those around you to reach new heights. Leadership is not about perfection, it's about progress. A constant evolution that, when embraced, creates a lasting impact.

Power Move

It's time to level-up! Download **The Leadership Effectiveness Level-Up** template from www.beinfluentialnow.com. (Password: **BINow2025**) (Case Sensitive). Using the strategies shared, reflect on your current leadership approach and outline what you will do differently to enhance your effectiveness.

THE MIRROR WITHIN: MASTERING SELF-AWARENESS AND EMOTIONAL INTELLIGENCE

> "
>
> Self-aware leaders take ownership in understanding how their personality traits, habits, and abilities affect their interactions with the people in their sphere of influence.
>
> ### DR. RHONDA L. ANDERSON
>
> "

A Leader's Transformation

A few years ago, I coached a leader named Samantha. She was confident and ambitious, but her team was underperforming. Morale was low, productivity had dropped significantly, and frustration was growing. When we first met, Samantha was unaware of the real reasons behind her team's struggles. She believed she had everything under control, but her team felt unheard and disrespected and believed their efforts were unappreciated.

Her lack of self-awareness and emotional intelligence was evident. During one of our early coaching sessions, she confidently declared, "I don't need to change—it's my team that needs to get it together." However, as we dug deeper, it became clear that her rigid leadership style, quick temper, and inability to listen were driving her team's disengagement. The respect they once had for her was eroding, and their lack of motivation was a direct reflection of her leadership approach.

Realizing she needed help, Samantha committed to a year of executive coaching. Over time, she experienced profound *lightbulb* moments. She began to change as she worked on developing self-awareness and emotional intelligence. She learned to listen actively, regulate her emotions, and adapt her approach to better support her team's needs. By the end of our coaching journey, Samantha had undergone a complete transformation. Her team was not only more effective but also more cohesive—and they genuinely respected her leadership. Samantha's relationships with her team members strengthened. The change was palpable, and it all stemmed from Samantha's willingness to look inward and grow as a leader.

Her story is a testament to the power of self-awareness. When leaders commit to personal growth their teams and organizations reap the benefits.

Why is Self-Leadership Important?

Self-leadership is the foundation of all other leadership abilities. Leaders who cannot effectively lead themselves will struggle to lead others. It requires self-awareness, self-discipline, and personal accountability. Leaders who master self-leadership set a powerful example for their teams, demonstrating that growth, responsibility, and development are lifelong commitments.

Without self-leadership, leaders risk making impulsive decisions, reacting emotionally to challenges, or becoming too rigid in their thinking. The most effective leaders engage in self-reflection, recognize their limitations, and actively seek ways to improve. By doing so, they cultivate a culture of continuous improvement within their teams.

Fostering Organizational Resilience and Adaptability

In today's unpredictable business landscape, volatility, uncertainty, complexity, and ambiguity are constant realities. For executives, the challenge is not only leading their teams through disruptions but also maintaining a strategic focus on long-term goals while fostering resilience and adaptability within their organizations.

Two essential leadership competencies that strengthen this capability are self-awareness and emotional intelligence (EQ). Leaders who are acutely aware of their strengths, limitations, emotions, and who can effectively understand and manage the emotions of the people on their teams, are better equipped to steer their organizations through challenging times.

Building Emotional Intelligence for Resilience

Empathy allows leaders to recognize how disruptions impact their employees on an emotional level. By acknowledging these feelings, executives can foster psychological safety, leading to a more resilient and adaptable workforce. Regular check-ins with team members, not just about work, but their well-being, can make a significant difference. Actively listening and validating their concerns, shows that emotional health is valued as much as productivity.

Another critical skill is emotional agility—the ability to recognize, understand, and respond to emotions effectively. Leaders with this ability make balanced decisions, even under pressure. In high-stress environments, managing both personal emotions and those of their teams is essential to maintaining focus on long-term goals. A useful technique for this is the "pause and reflect" method. Before making high-stakes decisions, take a moment to assess both the logical and emotional implications. Consider how your choice might impact team morale and the organization's ability to adapt in the long run.

By embracing self-awareness and emotional intelligence, executives can lead their teams through challenging times while maintaining strategic clarity. These leadership qualities enable resilience at both the individual and organizational levels, fostering an environment where adaptability and long-term success go hand in hand. Leaders who master these competencies will not only survive but thrive in today's complex business environment, achieving exceptional outcomes and driving peak team performance.

What Does it Mean to Be a Self-Aware Leader?

Being a self-aware leader means having a deep understanding of your own strengths, weaknesses, emotions, and the impact of your actions on others. It requires looking inward and acknowledging both your capabilities and areas for growth. A self-aware leader understands how their emotions and behavior affect their team's morale and performance.

I believe that leaders must actively address their weaknesses through self-awareness to foster authentic growth and build stronger relationships with their teams. When leaders lack self-awareness, they risk making decisions based on blind spots, which can erode trust and hinder team performance.

Being intentional about self-awareness allows leaders to recognize how their behaviors impact others and adjust accordingly, fostering a more positive and productive work environment. By confronting their weaknesses, leaders demonstrate humility and a commitment to continuous improvement—which, in turn, inspires their teams to do the same. Ultimately, self-aware leaders cultivate more cohesive, engaged, and high-performing teams. I challenge you to reflect on where you may have gaps in self-awareness as a leader. The five characteristics below provide a strong foundation for developing greater self-awareness.

Top Five Characteristics of a Self-Aware Leader

- **Reflectiveness:** Regularly reflects on decisions, behaviors, and leadership approaches to ensure alignment with values and goals.
- **Emotional Regulation:** Manages emotions effectively, avoiding impulsive reactions in high-stress situations.
- **Openness to Feedback:** Seeks feedback from teams and peers, embracing constructive criticism as an opportunity for growth.
- **Empathy:** Understands and responds to their team's emotional needs and dynamics, fostering a culture of support and psychological safety.
- **Adaptability:** Adjusts leadership style based on the needs of the situation and the team, demonstrating flexibility and responsiveness.

In moments of crisis, self-aware leaders regulate their emotions, preventing reactive decisions driven by fear or frustration. Self-regulation allows leaders to think more clearly, communicate more effectively, and maintain a steady presence, all of which are crucial for resilience. To enhance emotional awareness, develop a daily reflective practice such as journaling or mindfulness meditation. When faced with stress, pause and assess your emotions before making decisions to ensure you are responding rationally rather than impulsively.

A self-aware leader is also comfortable with vulnerability, demonstrating to their team that it's okay to admit uncertainty or seek guidance. By modeling adaptability, leaders foster a culture of openness and flexibility within their organizations. In team meetings, openly share instances where you've had to adjust your approach or when a plan didn't work, along with the lessons you learned. This level of transparency encourages others to embrace adaptability and resilience.

Accurately Assess Leadership Strengths & Weaknesses

———

Leaders who have a deep understanding of their personal strengths and weaknesses can effectively navigate disruptions more effectively by leveraging their strengths in times of crisis and seeking support in areas where they lack expertise. This promotes agility and adaptability within the leadership structure itself. Regularly conducting a personal SWOT (Strengths, Weaknesses, Opportunities, Threats) analysis helps leaders make informed decisions about growth areas and delegation strategies. Since challenges evolve over time, updating this assessment regularly ensures continuous development.

Self-awareness begins with knowing where you stand as a leader. Accurate self-assessment is key to identifying opportunities for growth. Many tools available in the marketplace to support this process, with 360-degree analysis being one of the most effective. This assessment provides insights from team members and peers, offering a well-rounded perspective on leadership strengths and areas of improvement.

Additionally, two of my favorite tools—the DISC Assessment and the CliftonStrengths Finder—provide deeper insights into leadership tendencies.

- ✦ **The DISC Assessment** categorizes behavior into four key types: **Dominance, Influence, Steadiness, and Conscientiousness.** This model helps leaders understand their **natural leadership style, communication preferences, and potential blind spots.** By highlighting how individuals interact with others, DISC enhances **communication, minimizes conflict, and fosters stronger team relationships.**

- ✦ **The CliftonStrengths Finder** focuses on **identifying and enhancing core talents** by categorizing **34 strengths into four domains: executing, influencing, relationship building, and strategic thinking.** By revealing a leader's **top five strengths**, this assessment encourages leaders to **focus on their natural abilities rather than solely working to improve weaknesses.**

Leveraging Leadership Assessments for Team Growth

My team and I specialize in conducting 360-degree feedback analyses and implementing both the DISC Assessment and CliftonStrengths Finder to help organizations maximize team performance.

We offer customized workshops and coaching sessions that guide leaders and teams in:

- Understanding their **DISC profiles** for improved communication and conflict resolution.
- Leveraging **CliftonStrengths** to **enhance leadership impact and team collaboration.**
- Aligning individual strengths with **organizational goals to drive business success**.

Our approach ensures that each team member understands how to contribute to the organization's success while enhancing their personal development. By integrating these tools, we empower leaders to build more cohesive, high-performing teams that drive results.

The Power of Presence:
Leading with Emotional Intelligence

Emotional intelligence (EQ) is the ability to understand, manage, and harness emotions, both in yourself and others. An emotionally intelligent leader recognizes that leadership is not just about tasks; it's about people. These leaders manage relationships with empathy, are aware of their emotional triggers, and inspire their teams—even in challenging times.

Leaders who lack emotional intelligence often struggle with interpersonal relationships, making it difficult to foster trust and cooperation within their teams. On the other hand, leaders with high EQ create a positive work environment where team members feel understood, valued, and motivated to perform at their best.

Top 5 Characteristics of an Emotionally Intelligent Leader

- ✦⁺ **Self-Awareness:** Self-awareness is the foundation to developing and enhancing your emotional intelligence. Recognize your emotions as they arise and understand how they influence your behavior, decision-making, and interactions with others.

- ✦⁺ **Self-Regulation:** As a leader, your reactions and actions are always being observed by your team. Maintaining control over your emotions, especially in high-pressure situations, builds credibility, trust, and stability within your team.

- ✦⁺ **Empathy:** Too often, I've seen leaders who are emotionally detached from their teams, treating them like robots rather than people. Leadership is not just about productivity; your team members are humans with emotions, personal lives, and challenges. Developing a deeper understanding of their perspectives fosters trust, loyalty, and engagement.

- ✦⁺ **Social Skills:** Your team plays a critical role in the success of your organization. Take time to build strong relationships with them by actively listening, maintaining clear lines of communication, and effectively managing conflict resolution.

- ✦⁺ **Motivation:** Maintain an optimistic attitude and inspire your team, even during tough times. When your organization faces challenges, your visibility and accessibility as a leader are crucial. Your energy and mindset set the tone for your team's resilience and morale.

How Leaders Can Improve Emotional Intelligence Within Their Teams

Improving emotional intelligence within a team requires a leader who actively promotes a culture of open communication, empathy, and understanding. One powerful tool I developed to support this is the *Collaborative Connection Blueprint*—a framework designed to help leaders and teams better understand one another's work styles, preferences, and communication habits.

The *Collaborative Connection Blueprint* is a comprehensive tool that outlines an individual's:

- Work style and preferences
- Communication approach
- Strengths and areas for growth

It provides a holistic view of how each team member operates, facilitating constructive dialogue that enhances collaboration.

Key Benefits of the Collaborative Connection Blueprint

- Enhances Communication & Collaboration – Reveals how team members prefer to interact, reducing misunderstandings and improving teamwork.
- Increases Self-Awareness – Helps individuals understand their work preferences and how they contribute to the team dynamic.
- Boosts Efficiency & Productivity – Provides clarity on team strengths, making projects and workflows more effective.
- Prevents & Resolves Conflicts – Promotes mutual understanding and respect, helping to resolve issues before they escalate.

I recommend that you and your team create a shared drive to store and update your **Collaborative Connection Blueprints**. Refer to them when you want to launch initiatives, leadership assignments, one-on-one meetings, recognition efforts, etc. This document should be treated as a living resource that can be updated as needed to support team dynamics and growth.

Self-Awareness & Emotional Intelligence: The Impact on Work-Life Balance for Leaders

Leaders often carry the weight of their team's success, which can lead to stress and burnout if not managed properly. Self-awareness and emotional intelligence are essential tools for maintaining work-life balance. A self-aware leader recognizes when they are approaching burnout and takes proactive steps to recharge. Emotionally intelligent leaders prioritize their well-being and model healthy boundaries for their teams, promoting a balanced work environment for everyone.

Below are strategies to help you and your team manage the demands of work and life more effectively together.

Strategies for Leaders to Manage Work-Life Balance and Avoid Burnout

- ✦ **Schedule Downtime for Strategic Thinking:** Leaders often get caught in the whirlwind of operations. Set aside dedicated time each week for uninterrupted reflection and strategic thinking. Creating this mental space, helps prioritize important tasks and reduces decision fatigue.

- ✦ **Use Energy-Based Task Prioritization:** Instead of focusing only on time management, align tasks with your natural energy levels. For example, reserving high-cognitive tasks for peak energy hours can lead to improve efficiency and reduce fatigue.

- ✦ **Take Micro-Retreats:** Incorporate brief mental "micro-retreats "or breaks throughout the day to reset your mind. Whether it's a 10-minute nature walk, short meditation, or creative journaling session, these pauses restore mental clarity and reduce burnout from constant decision-making.

- ✦ **Empower Delegation with Autonomy:** Delegation isn't just about handing off tasks, it's about empowering your team to make decisions. Giving employees autonomy reduces your workload while fostering trust, engagement, and professional growth.

- ✦ **Implement a Work-Life Integration Approach:** Rather than rigidly separating work and personal life, find ways to integrate both areas harmoniously. For example, flexible schedules or incorporating wellness activities during work hours reduce stress while maintaining high productivity. This balance helps leaders maintain a healthy boundary without feeling the need to "switch off" completely.

Foster a Healthy Team Culture

Leaders can help their teams maintain balance by implementing:

- ✦ Regular workload forecasting – Discuss upcoming tasks and redistribute as needed to prevent burnout.

- ✦ An "off switch" ritual – Encourage employees to establish a clear end-of-day routine.

- ✦ On-demand wellness days – Allow employees to take time off without stigma to recharge.

- ✦ Cross-team collaboration – Ensure workload coverage to support team members during personal time off.

By taking these steps, leaders create an environment that prioritizes well-being while sustaining performance.

Seven Strategies to Enhance Your Self-Awareness & Emotional Intelligence

Leaders who seek to elevate their influence and effectiveness must prioritize enhancing self-awareness and emotional intelligence. Understanding personal strengths, weaknesses, and leadership impact enables better-decision making, emotional regulation, and authentic leadership. When leaders are in tune with their emotions and motivations, they can build trust, navigate conflict with grace, and foster team cohesion. Self-aware leaders are better positioned to recognize blind spots in their leadership, allowing them to continuously grow and adapt in an ever-changing organizational landscape.

Emotional intelligence amplifies the leader's ability to connect with others, creating a culture where team members feel valued and understood. By understanding and managing their own emotions, emotionally intelligent leaders can guide their teams through challenges while maintaining a supportive, productive environment. As a result, teams are more likely to be engaged, motivated, and aligned with the organization's objectives. Ultimately, enhancing both self-awareness and emotional intelligence equips leaders to drive peak performance, increase employee satisfaction, and achieve exceptional outcomes.

1. **Practice Daily Reflection:** Take time each day to reflect on your actions, emotions, and decisions. Ask yourself what went well and where you can improve. Maintain an open mind, focus on growth, and set boundaries.

2. **Seek Feedback:** Regularly ask for constructive feedback from your team and peers. Be open to criticism and use it as a tool for personal growth.

3. **Develop Emotional Regulation Techniques:** Before reacting to challenges, pause and assess your emotions. Trust your intuition, but also practice mindfulness, deep breathing, or other stress-reduction techniques to maintain control in high-pressure situations.

4. **Strengthen Your Emotional Agility Muscle:** When facing a high-stakes decision, use the "pause and reflect" method. Take a moment to consider both logical and emotional impacts, evaluating how the decision will affect team morale, long-term resilience, and the organization's success.

5. **Cultivate Empathy:** Make a conscious effort to understand your team's emotions and perspectives. During conflicts or stressful situations, listen first, be quick to apologize, and be intentional about changing your behavior. Recognizing your personal triggers helps you respond thoughtfully rather than react emotionally.

6. **Invest in Personal Growth:** Take time to better understand yourself as a leader! Read books, attend workshops, take leadership assessments, and/or work with a coach to continuously enhance your leadership abilities and expand your perspective.

7. **Build Strong Relationships:** Leadership is about people. Be mindful of how you interact with your team members, both individually and as a group. Focus on building authenticity, trust, and connection to create an engaged and motivated team. The stronger your connections, the more effective you will be as a leader.

Dr. Rhonda's Leadership Lesson: Becoming a Self-Aware and Emotionally Intelligent Leader

Leadership is not just about driving results, it's about understanding yourself and your team on a deeper level. Becoming a self-aware and emotionally intelligent leader requires vulnerability, openness to change, and a commitment to continuous improvement. It's your responsibility as a leader to cultivate these qualities, not only for your success but for the success of your team. When you lead with self-awareness and emotional intelligence, you create a positive, high-performing environment where everyone can thrive.

By embracing self-awareness and emotional intelligence, you'll earn the trust and respect of your team, elevate productivity, and foster a workplace culture built on collaboration and growth. Your team will thank you for it, and your leadership will have a lasting, positive impact on both your organization and your own personal development.

 ## Power Move

Ready to improve your emotional intelligence? Download the Collaborative Connection Blueprint now. Visit www.beinfluentialnow.com to gain deeper insights into your work style and values. I highly recommend completing this activity with your team. (Password: **BINow2025**) (Case Sensitive)

VALUES IN ACTION: DEFINING YOUR LEADERSHIP COMPASS AND GOALS

"

Success in leadership starts with taking time to define personal leadership core values, develop goals that are aligned, and wholeheartedly live them out.

DR. RHONDA L. ANDERSON

"

Finding Direction in Values and Goals

Throughout my career, I can't tell you the number of times I have hosted leadership and management development cohorts only to discover that many leaders have never taken the time to establish their core leadership values or personal development goals. This, more often than not, is where the challenges arise. Leaders may excel in technical expertise but lack the self-awareness and clarity that comes from having clearly defined values and goals. Without these guiding principles, leaders risk misalignment within their teams, uncertainty in decision-making, and stagnation in their own professional growth. This is why I preach to leaders the importance of reflection—taking the time to define your core leadership values and set meaningful personal development goals. Doing so not only supports your personal growth but also establishes clear expectations for how you will lead and collaborate with your team. Your values and goals communicate to your sphere of influence who you are, what you stand for, and what you expect from them.

When you define your core values and leadership goals, you create a strong foundation for leadership to flourish. This foundation provides:

DIRECTION
Ensuring that your leadership approach remains intentional.

PURPOSE
Helping you stay aligned with what truly matters in your leadership journey.

ACCOUNTABILITY
Encouraging both you and your team to uphold shared principles.

Without this foundation, leadership becomes reactive rather than proactive, making it harder to build a cohesive, empowered team.

This chapter will guide you through the process of identifying and defining your core leadership values, developing personal leadership goals, and creating an Individual Development Plan (IDP) to support your growth and the growth of those you lead.

The Importance of Identifying Core Leadership Values

Core leadership values serve as the guiding principles that shape how you lead, make decisions, and interact with others. These values are not just abstract concepts, they are deeply ingrained beliefs that influence every aspect of your leadership. Identifying your core values is essential because they serve as your compass, ensuring consistency and integrity in your actions. When you are clear on your values, you are better able to make decisions that are aligned with who you are as a leader, and you inspire trust and confidence in your team.

Core values also help to set the tone for your leadership compass. As a leader, you have the power to shape the environment in which your team operates. When your values are clearly defined and articulated, your team members know what to expect from you, creating an environment of trust and stability. For example, if transparency is a core value, your team will understand that you prioritize open communication, and they will be more likely to follow suit. If accountability is a core value, it will foster a culture of ownership and responsibility, both for yourself and your team members.

By identifying and living by your core values, you create a leadership framework that fosters clarity, consistency, and empowerment within your team.

Leading with Intention:
The Power of Professional Development Goals

While core values provide the foundation for leadership, personal leadership development goals give direction and purpose. These goals are critical for continuous growth and self-improvement. Setting leadership goals is not just about advancing to a higher position or acquiring new skills; it's about becoming a more effective, impactful leader. Personal leadership goals help you focus on areas where you need to grow, whether it's improving emotional intelligence, enhancing communication skills, or developing strategic thinking.

Moreover, setting these goals allows you to track progress and hold yourself accountable. Just as we expect our teams to set and achieve performance goals, leaders must also challenge themselves to improve. This ongoing commitment to growth not only enhances your leadership abilities but also sets an example for your team. When your team sees that you are actively prioritizing your own development, they are more likely to invest in their own growth, creating a culture of continuous learning and improvement.

The Individual Development Plan (IDP): A Blueprint for Growth

An Individual Development Plan (IDP) is a formalized structure for setting and tracking your personal leadership development goals. It serves as a living document that outlines:

.+* Your leadership growth objectives

.+* The actions you will take to achieve them

.+* A timeline for completion

Having an IDP ensures that leadership growth is intentional, structured, and measurable rather than left to chance. It provides a clear roadmap for your development and reinforces accountability.

The benefits of an IDP are multifaceted.

.+* **For Leaders:** Provides structure, accountability, and a pathway to continuous improvement.

✦ **For Teams:** Communicates a commitment to personal growth, fostering a culture of learning and development.

✦ **For Organizations:** Encourages a mindset of self-improvement, engagement, and long-term success.

When leaders invest in their own growth, it encourages their team members to do the same, leading to higher engagement, productivity, and overall success.

An effective IDP should include SMART (Specific, Measurable, Attainable, Relevant, and Time-bound) goals. These goals might focus on areas such as improving leadership communication, strengthening emotional intelligence, or building better relationships with team members. Each goal should have clear action steps, such as attending leadership workshops, seeking mentorship, or reading leadership literature. Regularly reviewing and updating your IDP ensures that you stay on track and allows you to adjust your goals as needed.

Cultivating a Growth Mindset to Continuously Improve Your Leadership Abilities

One of the most important qualities a leader can cultivate is a growth mindset—the belief that abilities and intelligence can be developed through dedication, hard work, and learning from mistakes. Leaders who embrace this mindset are more likely to take risks, seek feedback, and push beyond their comfort zones to improve their skills.

Cultivating a growth mindset enables leaders to view setbacks as learning experiences for growth rather than obstacles. It allows you to embrace failure as a learning experience and seek out ways to continuously improve your leadership abilities. With a growth mindset, you are more likely to invest in your own development and encourage your team members to do the same. This creates a culture of learning and adaptability, which is essential in today's fast-paced and ever-changing work environment.

Five Strategies for Defining Your Leadership Core Values & Setting Personal Leadership Development Goals

Remember, defining your leadership core values is essential for guiding decision-making and fostering consistency in your leadership approach. When your actions align with your core values, you set a clear standard that inspires trust and loyalty within your team. Establishing personal leadership development goals helps you grow continuously, adapt to new challenges, and ensure purpose-driven leadership. These goals not only keep you focused on self-improvement but also model a growth mindset for your team. Ultimately, identifying your core values and setting meaningful goals is the foundation for authentic, impactful leadership.

Here are five strategies to help you define your core values and create your personal leadership goals:

1. **Identify Your Top Five Core Values:** Start by identifying the five values that are most important to you as a leader. Consider what principles guide your decisions and interactions. Engage in a values clarification activity to help prioritize what matters most.

   Ask yourself:

   ✦ Do I value innovation, transparency, accountability, or collaboration?

   ✦ How do these values shape my leadership style?

   Once identified, take time to reflect on how your values show up in your leadership.

2. **Articulate Your Values to Your Team:** Once you've defined your values, communicate them clearly to your team. Let them know:

   ✦ What you stand for as a leader

   ✦ How these values will shape your leadership style and team culture.

   Clear communication creates alignment between your actions and expectations, builds trust, and ensures your team understands your expectations.

3. **Integrate Your Values into Your Decision-Making:** Ensure that your values are not just theoretical but are integrated into your daily actions and decisions.

   ✦ Pause and reflect on whether your decisions align with your core values.

   ✦ Hold yourself accountable to act in ways that are aligned with your values.

   This not only strengthens your leadership credibility but also sets a powerful example for your team.

4. **Create an Individual Development Plan (IDP) and Commit to Your Goals:** Develop a detailed IDP that outlines:

   ✦ Your leadership development goals.

   ✦ Specific actions you will take to improve in these areas that align with your core values.

   ✦ A timeline for tracking progress to ensure you are making headway.

   Consistency is key—commit to working on your goals daily.

5. **Re-evaluate, Refine, and Celebrate Wins:** Leadership development is an ongoing process. Periodically re-evaluate your core values and goals to ensure they still align with your leadership journey.

   ✦ Adjust your goals as your leadership journey evolves.

   ✦ Celebrate your progress. Recognizing small wins keeps you motivated and reinforces your commitment to growth.

Dr. Rhonda's Leadership Lesson: The Foundation of Authentic Leadership

Developing and embodying core leadership values and personal leadership goals is the foundation of authentic, purpose-driven leadership. When you lead with clarity of values and a commitment to growth, you inspire others to follow. This builds trust and empowers your team to achieve greatness. By continuously reflecting on your values and striving to improve, you not only elevate your own leadership abilities but also create a ripple effect that elevates those around you. True leadership is not about perfection but about progression,

When you define your values and set meaningful personal goals, you set the stage for a lasting impact.

 ## Power Move

It's time to define your core leadership values and set your personal leadership development goals. Download *the **Core Leadership Values*** template and the ***Individual Development Plan*** **(IDP)** at www.beinfluentialnow.com. (Password: **BINow2025**) (Case Sensitive)

I highly recommend using these tools to identify your leadership values and completing these exercises with your team.

THE TRUST EQUATION: BUILDING UNSHAKABLE LEADERSHIP FOUNDATIONS

"

Remember, trust plays a vital role in the foundation of leadership and must be present in order to achieve optimal team cohesion and effectiveness.

DR. RHONDA L. ANDERSON

"

Earning Trust, Step by Step

Thinking back, I vividly remember one of my first leadership roles. As a new employee, I was immediately tasked with managing several high-stakes projects. I had to hit the ground running, and I quickly realized that gaining my manager's trust would be a significant challenge. For months, I worked tirelessly, implementing projects successfully, performing at high levels, and navigating the demands of my position. Yet, it took nearly ten months before I felt like I had truly earned her trust. During that time, I constantly felt like I was walking on thin ice. One misstep, and it could all fall apart. My stress levels were through the roof because I knew there was no room for error. Reflecting on that experience, I get it: trust is incredibly hard to earn but even harder to regain once it's broken.

As a leader, building trust with your team is essential. Each team member was hired for their skills, experience, and potential. Trusting them to perform at optimal levels is not just a luxury; it's a necessity. When you trust your team, you free yourself to focus on strategic leadership rather than micromanagement. However, building that trust doesn't happen overnight. It takes time, effort, and consistency. Just as it took time for my manager to trust me, leaders must remember that earning employees' trust is a two-way street. It must be nurtured, and it requires a foundation of integrity, transparency, and mutual respect.

Defining Trust for Leaders & the Obstacles They Face

At its core, trust is the belief in a person's reliability, integrity, and competence. For leaders, trust extends beyond mere competence; it encompasses the willingness to be vulnerable and authentic, allowing others to believe in your leadership. Trust is not something leaders can demand. It must be earned through consistent actions, sound decisions, and genuine care for the well-being of your team.

Leaders often face barriers when trying to build and maintain trust. Here are a few common challenges:

- **Perceived Hierarchy:** Team members may feel disconnected from leadership due to positional authority, making trust-building more difficult.

- **Lack of Communication:** Inconsistent messaging or failure to be transparent can erode trust over time.

- **Fear of Failure:** Leaders sometimes hesitate to fully trust their teams due to past experiences, fear of mistakes, or an overemphasis on control.

- **Organizational Changes:** Rapid changes without clear leadership guidance can lead to uncertainty and mistrust.

- **Inconsistent Leadership Behavior:** If leaders say one thing but do another, trust deteriorates quickly.

Although these challenges are common, they can and must be overcome—because trust is the cornerstone of all effective leadership.

Why It's Important to Be a Trustworthy Leader

Being a trustworthy leader has far-reaching benefits for both the leader and the team. Trust increases productivity, collaboration, and morale, while reducing conflicts and the need for constant oversight. When team members trust their leader, they feel more confident in their roles and are willing to take initiative, share ideas, and go above and beyond to contribute to the team's success.

A trustworthy leader fosters an environment of psychological safety, where team members feel empowered to take risks, innovate, and contribute without fear of retribution. Trustworthy leaders also model accountability and transparency, setting the standard for how the entire team operates. In organizations where trust is high, employees are more engaged, retention rates improve, and innovation thrives. In short, trust accelerates performance, deepens relationships, and creates a culture where both leaders and team members can flourish.

Building Trust in Onsite, Hybrid, and Remote Teams

The dynamics of trust-building can vary significantly depending on whether a team is working onsite, in a hybrid setup, or remotely. While trust is essential in all of these environments, the challenges differ, requiring leaders to adapt their approach accordingly.

Onsite Teams

In traditional, onsite teams, leaders and employees interact face-to-face, allowing for more direct communication and relationship-building. While this setup makes it easier to build trust through daily interactions, it can also create challenges—especially if leaders micromanage or fail to demonstrate trust in their team members' abilities. Best practices for building trust in an onsite environment include fostering open communication, being approachable, and empowering team members to make decisions.

Hybrid Teams

In hybrid teams, where some employees work onsite and others remotely, the biggest challenge is ensuring remote employees feel equally trusted and valued as their onsite counterparts. Leaders must be intentional about creating a sense of inclusion and fairness in a hybrid setup. This can be done by maintaining open lines of communication with all team members, regardless of their location, and ensuring that opportunities for growth and recognition are available to everyone. Regular check-ins, virtual team-building activities, and a clear structured approach to collaboration can help create balance and maintain trust in hybrid teams.

Remote Teams

Remote teams—now more common than ever—pose unique trust-building challenges. Without in-person interaction, it's easy for team members to feel disconnected from their leader and colleagues. In this setting, trust must be built on a foundation of communication, accountability, and autonomy. Leaders should focus on creating a strong virtual culture by fostering regular communication through video calls, team meetings, and one-on-one check-ins. Providing clarity on expectations and allowing remote workers the autonomy to manage their workload also goes a long way in building trust.

In all three environments, the key to overcoming challenges is clear, transparent communication and a willingness to trust your team to perform at their best, regardless of physical proximity.

How to Build Trust with New Employees

Building trust with new employees is a critical part of the onboarding process. New hires are often eager to prove themselves but they may feel uncertain about their place in the team and how much autonomy they have. As a leader, it's your job to create a welcoming and supportive environment that fosters trust from the very beginning.

Start by being transparent about your expectations and providing clear guidance on how their role fits into the larger team and organizational objectives. Open communication is key—make yourself available for questions, provide constructive feedback, and show genuine interest in their success. Additionally, small actions like acknowledging their contributions, celebrating early wins, and involving them in team discussions can go a long way in building rapport and trust. Another important aspect is giving new employees opportunities to demonstrate their abilities early on. By delegating meaningful tasks and giving them room to shine, you not only build their confidence but also show that you trust them.

By showing trust in new employees early on, you encourage them to reciprocate that trust in you as their leader.

Do You Know If Your Team Trusts You as a Leader?—How to Find Out

Trust is not always easy to measure, but there are clear indicators that can reveal whether your team trusts you as a leader. One of the most telling signs is how open and comfortable team members feel when communicating with you. Do your team members feel comfortable sharing their ideas, concerns, or feedback with you without hesitation? If so, that's a strong indicator that they trust you. If team members avoid difficult conversations or hesitate to speak up, it may indicate a lack of trust.

Another indicator is how your team responds to challenges. Do they remain engaged and solution-oriented when faced with obstacles, or do they retreat, waiting for you to make all the decisions? When a team trusts its leader, they are more likely to take ownership of problems and work collaboratively to solve them. If they become disengaged or wait for direction instead of taking initiative, it may be a sign that they do not feel secure in their leadership environment.

Seeking direct feedback is one of the most effective ways to gauge trust from your team. Conducting anonymous surveys or holding one-on-one conversations allows employees to share their thoughts openly about how they feel about your leadership. Be open to hearing both positive and constructive feedback and be willing to make changes if necessary. By showing that you value their opinions and are committed to improving, you create a workplace culture that reinforces the trust they have in you.

Ten Strategies for Building Trust As A Leader

Building trust requires consistent effort and intentional actions. Here are ten strategies leaders can use to build trust with their teams:

1. **Be Transparent & Honest:** Share information openly with your team, whether it's about business decisions, challenges, or successes. Transparency fosters trust by showing that you have nothing to hide. Focus on leading with empathy and authenticity to build deeper connections.

2. **Follow Through on Commitments:** Be reliable! Trust is built when leaders do what they say they will do. If you make a promise or commitment to your team, ensure that you follow through. Your consistency and dependability will reinforce their confidence in you.

3. **Communicate Regularly and Clearly:** Keep the lines of communication open and ensure that your messages are clear and understood. Prioritize regular updates, team meetings, one-on-one check-ins, and open discussions to build trust over time.

4. **Delegate Responsibility:** Show trust in your team by delegating important tasks and giving them the autonomy to make decisions. This empowers them, demonstrates that you have confidence in their abilities, and value their contributions.

5. **Acknowledge Mistakes & Learn From Losses:** When you make a mistake, own up to it. Admitting when you are wrong shows humility and authenticity, both of which strengthen trust. Learn from losses together as a team and create a culture where mistakes are learning opportunities, not something to hold over your employee's heads.

6. **Give Constructive Feedback:** Provide feedback that helps your team grow. Be honest yet supportive. Constructive feedback builds trust by showing that you are invested in their success.

7. **Create a Safe Environment for Risk-Taking:** Encourage innovation by fostering a culture where team members feel safe to take risks and share new ideas. Trust grows when people know they won't be penalized for trying something new.

8. **Model the Behavior You Expect:** As a leader, your actions set the standard for your team. Demonstrate the integrity, professionalism, and empathy you expect from others. Be considerate of the needs of your employees, especially when they are experiencing life challenges.

9. **Celebrate Wins:** Recognize both individual and team accomplishments. Celebrating wins shows your team that you value their contributions, reinforcing a culture of appreciation and trust.

10. **Be Accessible and Approachable:** Make yourself available to your team. Whether they have concerns, questions, or ideas, knowing that you are approachable fosters an environment of openness and trust. Consider hosting regular off-site team-building activities to strengthen relationships.

 Dr. Rhonda's Leadership Lesson: Trust is the Foundation of Team Success

Building trust with your team is not a one-time effort—it's an ongoing process that requires patience, consistency, and authenticity. Trust is the foundation of all successful leadership, and without it, even the most talented teams can falter. When trust is present, communication flows freely, collaboration thrives, and your team is empowered to take ownership of their roles and contribute to the organization's success.

As a leader, your ability to cultivate trust will determine the strength and longevity of your team's performance. Lead with integrity, be transparent, and demonstrate your confidence in your team. In return, you will build a culture of mutual respect, accountability, and excellence that will drive your team to achieve greatness.

 Power Move

Download the ***Trust Mapping: A Leader's Guide to Fostering Trust*** template at www.beinfluentialnow.com to identify the top 3-6 actions you will take to build or enhance trust within your team. (Password: **BINow2025**) (Case Sensitive)

THE ART OF INFLUENCE: COMMUNICATION TACTICS THAT TRANSFORM TEAMS

> " Intentionally create a fear-free space where your team can communicate the good, the bad, and the ugly with you.
>
> **DR. RHONDA L. ANDERSON** "

Effective communication is the heartbeat of successful leadership. It allows leaders to convey their vision, align teams with common goals, and foster collaboration in a way that drives progress. Yet, despite its critical role, communication is often one of the most overlooked leadership skills. In this chapter, we will explore communication strategies that leaders can use to inspire their teams, navigate challenges, and achieve extraordinary results.

The Power of Opening the Door: A Story of Missed Opportunities

I once had a colleague who, despite her wealth of experience and innovative thinking, never spoke up during our team meetings. Week after week, she sat silently as we brainstormed ideas and discussed strategies, though her mind was brimming with insights that could have transformed our projects. Our manager, though effective in many ways, never directly invited her to contribute. She was a team member who needed a little encouragement to share her thoughts, but instead, she was consistently overlooked.

Over time, she began to feel invisible. Doubting her value to the team, she started withdrawing—not just from meetings, but from her work as well. The meetings she once found interesting now filled her with dread, as she started to believe that her voice didn't matter. Eventually, her enthusiasm waned, and her contributions—both in meetings and outside of them—began to dwindle.

This scenario is not uncommon. Leaders often unintentionally stifle voices that could add tremendous value simply because they don't actively create space for those contributions. It becomes a self-perpetuating cycle—employees don't speak because they feel unheard, and leaders assume they have nothing to contribute because they remain silent.

Empowering employees to share their knowledge and perspectives is essential for innovation and team performance. Leaders must recognize that communication isn't just about what is said—it's about ensuring that every member of the team feels they have the opportunity to speak and be heard. Opening the door to communication is a leader's responsibility, and doing so can transform a silent observer into a key driver of team success.

What Is Effective Communication?

Effective communication is not merely the exchange of information—it's about ensuring that the message is understood, acted upon, and ultimately leads to meaningful progress. In leadership, effective communication goes beyond giving orders or delivering instructions. It requires creating an environment where dialogue is encouraged, ideas are shared freely, and every member of the team feels respected.

Key Elements of Effective Communication in Leadership

- **Clarity & Simplicity:** Messages should be clear, concise, and free of unnecessary jargon to ensure easy comprehension.
- **Active Listening:** Leaders must listen to both what is said and what is left unspoken, demonstrating that they genuinely value their team's input.
- **Adaptability:** Different team members respond to different communication styles. Adapting your approach improves connection and engagement.
- **Constructive Feedback:** Providing timely, actionable feedback fosters trust and growth. Leaders who communicate honestly and supportively build stronger teams.
- **Two-Way Communication:** Encouraging open dialogue creates an environment where employees feel safe sharing their thoughts, concerns, and ideas.

When leaders prioritize intentional, open, and transparent communication, they build teams that are stronger, more engaged, and better positioned for success.

The Importance of Communication as a Leader

Leadership is as much about communication as it is about vision and strategy. Even the most well-crafted strategy will fail if it's not communicated effectively. The ability to articulate your vision, set clear expectations, and provide meaningful feedback is what enables you to bring others along with you on the journey toward success.

Effective communication serves as the cornerstone of strong leadership, driving clarity, fostering collaboration, and boosting team morale. Clear communication ensures everyone understands their roles, responsibilities, and goals, preventing misunderstandings that could derail even the most skilled teams. Open dialogue builds trust, which is the foundation of successful collaboration and idea-sharing. When leaders communicate transparently, employees feel valued, leading to a boost in their morale and engagement. Additionally, strong communication channels enable leaders to resolve conflicts quickly and constructively, maintaining team cohesion. Finally, fostering open communication allows for diverse perspectives, leading to more informed decision-making and better outcomes.

Communicating with On-Site, Virtual, and Hybrid Teams: Strategies for Success

In today's workplace, teams can be structured in various ways: on-site, virtual, or hybrid settings. Each environment presents unique communication challenges, and leaders must adapt their communication strategies to ensure cohesion and productivity.

On-Site Teams

On-site teams benefit from face-to-face interactions where non-verbal cues help build rapport and trust. However, over-reliance on in-person meetings can sometimes lead to slow productivity, and informal communication may cause important messages to be overlooked. Here are a few strategies to enhance communication with on-site teams:

- ✦ **Regular Stand-Ups:** Short, structured daily or weekly meetings to align team members and clarify priorities.

- ✦ **Be Mindful of Non-verbal Cues:** Pay attention to body language and tone to gauge understanding and engagement.

- ✦ **Create Open-door Policies:** Ensure employees feel comfortable coming to you with questions, concerns, or feedback at any time.

Virtual Teams

With virtual teams, communication must be more intentional. The absence of face-to-face interaction can lead to misunderstandings, feelings of isolation, or a disconnect from the broader team. Check out the list of strategies below to enhance communication with virtual teams:

- ✦ **Schedule Frequent Check-Ins:** Frequent video or phone calls help remote employees feel connected and supported.

- ✦ **Clear Written Communication:** Since most communication happens via email or messaging platforms, clarity in written communication is crucial.

- ✦ **Leverage Collaborative Tools:** Platforms like Slack, Microsoft Teams, or Asana can help track projects and maintain real-time communication.

Hybrid Teams

Hybrid teams, which blend on-site and remote employees, require a balance of communication methods. Leaders must ensure that remote workers don't feel excluded and that on-site workers aren't overwhelmed by constant communication. Quickly enhance communication with hybrid teams by utilizing these three strategies:

- ✦ **Equal Participation:** In meetings, ensure that both in-person and remote employees have equal opportunities to contribute.

- ✦ **Unified Communication Platforms:** Use digital tools that allow seamless communication between on-site and remote team members to prevent information gaps.

.✦⁺ **Inclusion Efforts:** Make an intentional effort to engage remote employees in informal conversations and decision-making processes.

Communicating with Multiple Generations in the Workplace

The modern workplace often consists of multiple generations, each with distinct communication preferences and expectations. Understanding these differences is essential for leading a diverse team effectively:

.✦⁺ **Traditionalists (Born before 1946)**

Communication Style: Prefer formal, top-down communication and value respect for authority.

Strategy: Use structured, formal communication and acknowledge their experience and contributions.

.✦⁺ **Baby Boomers (1946–1964)**

Communication Style: Favor face-to-face communication and expect personal interaction.

Strategy: Be personable and provide opportunities for one-on-one dialogue.

.✦⁺ **Generation X (1965–1980)**

Communication Style: Prefer concise, direct communication and value efficiency.

Strategy: Avoid micromanaging; focus on clear, outcome-based communication.

.✦⁺ **Millennials (1981–1996)**

Communication Style: Value collaboration and feedback and are comfortable with digital communication.

Strategy: Use collaborative tools and provide regular feedback to maintain engagement.

.+⁺ **Generation Z (1997 and beyond)**
Communication Style: Highly visual and digital, preferring real-time feedback.
Strategy: Leverage technology and social platforms for communication, and provide instant feedback and recognition.

By adapting communication styles to fit generational preferences, leaders can maximize engagement, collaboration, and team performance.

Managing Conflict to Maintain Cohesion in On-Site, Virtual, and Hybrid Teams

Conflict is inevitable in any team, but how leaders approach it can either harm or enhance team cohesion. Effective communication is essential to resolving conflicts quickly and maintaining a positive, collaborative work environment.

Managing conflict effectively requires a proactive and thoughtful approach. Addressing issues early is essential, as letting conflicts fester can lead to escalation and strained team dynamics. Leaders should create an environment where open dialogue is encouraged, allowing team members to express concerns constructively. When mediating, it's crucial to remain neutral, focusing on solutions that benefit the entire team rather than taking sides. Additionally, leaders must tailor their conflict resolution strategies to the work environment—particularly in virtual settings, where misunderstandings can arise more easily. Handling conflicts through video or phone calls rather than text or email can help minimize miscommunication and foster clearer resolutions.

Five Strategies to Enhance Communication as a Leader

Leaders must be intentional about improving their communication because how they communicate directly impacts team performance, trust, and engagement. When leaders prioritize effective communication, they create an environment where team members feel heard, valued, and aligned with the organization's goals. Intentional communication fosters clarity, reducing misunderstandings and confusion that could lead to mistakes or disengagement.

It also strengthens relationships, as leaders who communicate thoughtfully build trust and rapport with their teams. By continuously refining their communication skills, leaders become more adaptable to diverse team dynamics and can navigate challenges with confidence, ultimately driving better results and stronger team cohesion. Here are five strategies you can use to enhance your communication skills:

1. **Be Transparent:** Transparency builds trust. Share information openly with your team, especially during times of uncertainty. Keeping employees informed fosters confidence and ensures alignment with organizational objectives.

2. **Encourage Feedback:** Create an environment where feedback flows both ways—this not only improves communication but also helps you grow as a leader by gaining valuable insights from your team.

3. **Adapt to Different Styles:** Not everyone communicates the same way. Adapt your style to fit the needs and preferences of your team members. Recognizing and adjusting to different styles improves clarity, engagement, and collaboration.

4. **Use Storytelling:** Stories are a powerful tool for conveying vision and inspiring action. Use storytelling to illustrate points, make complex ideas more relatable, and connect with your team on an emotional level.

5. **Practice Empathy:** Empathy is at the core of effective communication.

Understanding the perspectives and emotions of your team members creates more meaningful and supportive conversations.

 ## Dr. Rhonda's Leadership Lesson: Reflect on Your Communication Style

Every interaction you have with your team is an opportunity to build trust, inspire action, and reinforce your leadership. However, poor communication can erode your reputation if communication is handled poorly. Reflect regularly on your communication style, seeking feedback from your team to ensure you're fostering an environment of openness, collaboration, and trust.

Leadership isn't just about speaking—it's about listening, adapting, and ensuring that everyone on your team feels heard and valued. Communication is your most powerful tool as a leader. Use it wisely.

 ## Power Move

Download the ***Mastering Leadership Communication: A Self-Assessment*** at www.beinfluentialnow.com to evaluate your communication skills as a leader.

(Password: **BINow2025**) (Case Sensitive)

THE SAFETY NET: NURTURING PSYCHOLOGICAL SAFETY AND TEAM BELONGING

> "
>
> Mastering the art of psychological safety and cultivating a supportive team environment is necessary in order for you to become an influential leader.
>
> DR. RHONDA L. ANDERSON
>
> "

Creating a psychologically safe, inclusive, and supportive team environment is no longer optional; it's a leadership imperative. Without these elements, even the most talented teams can struggle to reach their full potential. Leaders must intentionally foster an environment where team members feel secure in expressing their thoughts and ideas, knowing that they won't face retaliation, ridicule, or alienation.

This chapter delves into the importance of psychological safety, diversity, equity, and inclusion (DEI) in leadership and provides strategies for cultivating an environment where everyone feels valued and empowered to contribute.

A Leadership Crisis:
Ignoring Psychological Safety and Inclusion

I once worked with a client, a vice president at a large organization, who was faced with a daunting challenge. The company's high-pressure culture disregarded emotional intelligence and lacked a supportive team environment. Team members could behave disrespectfully toward one another without fear of repercussions, and discriminatory practices were quietly tolerated. The office was a battleground of stress, where employees were too afraid to speak up, fearing that their honesty would cost them their jobs or any chance of promotion.

The leadership team in this organization had lost control. They avoided difficult conversations, reluctant to confront their peers or hold anyone accountable for inappropriate behavior or poor performance. The result? The team's core values, if they had any, became meaningless. Leaders were paralyzed by fear, unwilling to address the hostile and unhealthy culture that was driving their best people to disengage or leave.

The turning point came when my client realized that, as a leader, ignoring the issue was no longer an option. Leaders must take responsibility for creating and maintaining an environment where psychological safety is not just encouraged but expected. Core values, when genuinely upheld, serve as the guiding framework that define acceptable behavior and ensure that the workplace is one where every individual feels secure, respected, and valued.

Safe Spaces, Strong Teams: The Power of Psychological Safety

Psychological safety, a term coined by Harvard professor Amy Edmondson, refers to the belief that one can speak up, share ideas, ask questions, and admit mistakes without fear of being punished or humiliated. In psychologically safe environments, employees feel comfortable bringing their whole selves to work, knowing that their contributions will be respected and that mistakes are seen as learning opportunities, not failures. It is important for leaders to keep psychological safety top of mind and actively demonstrate their commitment to psychological safety to show their teams they are serious about fostering a safe environment. Promoting psychological safety in leadership can have many benefits:

- ✦ **Promotes Innovation:** When team members feel safe to share their ideas, even bold ones, it opens the door to creativity and innovation.
- ✦ **Boosts Engagement:** Employees who feel valued and respected are more likely to stay engaged in their work.
- ✦ **Enhances Collaboration:** Psychological safety fosters open communication, which strengthens teamwork, collaboration, and effective problem-solving.
- ✦ **Reduces Turnover:** People are more likely to stay in organizations where they feel psychologically safe and included.

Psychological safety is necessary across all types of teams, whether on-site, remote, or hybrid. Each environment presents unique challenges, but leaders who prioritize psychological safety can create an inclusive atmosphere in any workplace.

On-site teams benefit from face-to-face interactions but can still be vulnerable to toxic workplace dynamics. If hierarchical structures discourage input or if team members fear speaking up, psychological safety is compromised.

Leadership Action:

- ✦ Foster open-door policies to encourage honest conversations.
- ✦ Set clear behavioral expectations to prevent toxic work environments.

Remote teams face the challenge of isolation, which can make team members feel disconnected and hesitant to speak up. Leaders must intentionally create virtual spaces where individuals feel included and heard.

Leadership Action:

- ✦ Create virtual spaces where employees feel included (e.g., video check-ins, collaborative platforms).
- ✦ Ensure equal opportunities for remote employees to contribute during meetings.

Hybrid teams blend remote and on-site employees, creating unique challenges. Remote employees may feel excluded from key conversations, while on-site employees may feel overloaded with communication responsibilities. Leaders need to ensure that remote team members aren't forgotten or marginalized in these hybrid environments.

Leadership Action:

- ✦ Be intentional about inclusion by giving remote employees a voice in decision-making.
- ✦ Use consistent communication tools to bridge the gap between remote and in-person workers.

By prioritizing psychological safety across all work environments, leaders create teams that are engaged, collaborative, and empowered to perform at their best.

The Role of Diversity, Equity, and Inclusion (DEI) in Effective Leadership

Diversity, equity, and inclusion (DEI) are integral for creating psychologically safe and supportive team environments. DEI goes beyond just meeting diversity quotas—it's about recognizing the unique experiences, backgrounds, and perspectives each individual brings to the table and ensuring that all voices are heard and valued.

Leaders who prioritize DEI are positioned to drive significant organizational success. By embracing DEI, leaders can enhance team performance, as diverse teams bring a broader spectrum of perspectives, leading to better decision-making and outcomes. Fostering an inclusive environment also fuels innovation, as diverse thoughts encourage fresh ideas and creative problem-solving. Additionally, when team members feel valued and included, they are more likely to collaborate and support one another, strengthening team cohesion and alignment toward shared goals.

Conversely, leaders who fail to integrate DEI into their leadership style risk creating environments where only certain voices are heard, leaving others feeling excluded or marginalized. This not only stifles innovation but also creates resentment and disengagement among team members, weakening morale.

Leaders Build Inclusive Teams

Building an inclusive team requires more than just good intentions. Leaders must actively create an environment where every team member feels valued, respected, and empowered to contribute. Here are a few strategies for building inclusive teams:

- ✦ **Establish Clear Values and Expectations:** Set the tone for inclusion by clearly defining the team's core values—respect, collaboration, and open communication. Make it clear that disrespect or exclusionary behavior will not be tolerated.

- ✦ **Be Intentional About Representation:** Ensure that your team reflects a range of perspectives, backgrounds, and experiences. Seek out diverse talent and ensure that everyone has equal opportunities for growth and advancement.

- ✦ **Facilitate Open Dialogue:** Encourage honest conversations about inclusivity and be open to feedback from your team on how you can improve. Make it clear that every voice matters.

- ✦ **Educate Yourself and Your Team:** Commit to continuously educating yourself and your team on unconscious bias and other barriers to inclusivity. Invest in training and resources that foster a deeper understanding of DEI issues.

Why Leaders Need to Build a Supportive Team Environment

A supportive team environment is one where team members feel safe, respected, and valued. In such an environment, people are more likely to collaborate, take risks, and go the extra mile to achieve shared goals.

A supportive team environment is crucial because it fosters trust, which is the foundation for collaboration, innovation, and overall team success. When employees feel supported, their engagement and investment in their work increase, leading to higher levels of productivity. Additionally, a supportive environment enhances employees' mental and emotional well-being, reducing burnout and turnover, which contributes to a healthier, more resilient team dynamic.

Leaders can create a supportive environment by showing empathy, which is key to understanding and acknowledging team members' emotions, challenges, and successes, fostering deeper connections and loyalty. Offering regular recognition and encouragement reinforces a culture of support and appreciation. Encouraging work-life balance is also essential, as it helps reduce stress and prevent burnout by promoting healthy work habits. Lastly, leaders set the tone for the team by modeling positive behavior and consistently demonstrating the supportive, respectful, and inclusive conduct they expect from others in every interaction.

Seven Strategies for Mastering Psychological Safety & Cultivating a Supportive Team Environment

Mastering psychological safety and cultivating a supportive team environment requires ongoing effort and intentionality. Below are seven key strategies to help leaders build a strong, supportive team environment.

1. **Establish Clear Behavioral Norms:** Define acceptable and unacceptable behaviors and set clear expectations for how team members should interact with one another. Be transparent about the consequences of violating these norms.

2. **Lead by Example:** Model the behavior you want to see from your team. If you want your team to be open, respectful, and inclusive, demonstrate these qualities in your daily interactions. Show respect, openness, and vulnerability. Admit your mistakes when appropriate. This signals to your team that it's safe for them to do the same.

3. **Create Opportunities for Open Dialogue:** Regularly check in with your team, both individually and as a group, to discuss any concerns, ideas, or feedback. Facilitate structured discussions, such as anonymous surveys or listening sessions, to encourage honest input from team members who may be hesitant to speak up in group settings.

4. **Hold Team Members Accountable:** When team members behave in ways that undermine psychological safety or inclusivity, address the issue promptly and fairly. Be clear about the consequences of harmful behavior and ensure that everyone understands the importance of upholding the team's core values.

5. **Encourage Diversity of Thought:** Actively seek out diverse perspectives and create space for alternative viewpoints. Encourage team members to challenge assumptions and offer new ideas without fear of judgment for healthy debate and innovation. Recognize and reward innovative thinking, even if not all ideas lead to immediate results, welcoming ideas without fear of judgement.

6. **Provide Continuous Support:** Be available and approachable, both in formal and informal settings. Whether through regular one-on-one meetings or an open-door policy, make sure your team knows you're there to support them. Offer resources such as mentorship, professional development, and mental health support to ensure your team have what they need to thrive and create a sense of security and trust.

7. **Build Psychological Resilience:** Equip your team with the skills and mindset needed to navigate challenges and setbacks. This includes encouraging growth through failure and problem-solving, fostering an attitude of learning from mistakes. Promote a culture of continuous improvement, where team members feel motivated to push themselves and each other to reach new heights.

Dr. Rhonda's Leadership Lesson: The Power of Psychological Safety and Inclusion

As leaders, we are responsible for the environments we create. It's not enough to drive for results; we must also ensure that the path to those results is paved with respect, support, and inclusivity. Every interaction with your team is an opportunity to either build or erode psychological safety.

Leaders who foster psychologically safe and inclusive environments understand that diversity of thought, respect for individual experiences, and open communication are critical for success. By promoting these values, we create the conditions for innovation, engagement, and peak performance. By embracing diverse perspectives and fostering a culture of trust and belonging, we strengthen the resilience and cohesion of our teams, ensuring that they can thrive in any environment.

 ## Power Move

Download the *Culture of Care Audit* template at www.beinfluentialnow.com to reflect on ways to enhance psychological safety and foster a supportive team culture.

(Password: **BINow2025**) (Case Sensitive)

ALIGNED FOR IMPACT: BRIDGING TEAM GOALS WITH VISIONARY OBJECTIVES

> 66
>
> When you take time to align your team's objectives with the organization's vision, you create a powerful synergy that drives collective team success, fosters a sense of purpose, and turns individual efforts into transformative outcomes.
>
> **DR. RHONDA L. ANDERSON**
>
> 99

In leadership, one of the most critical components for success is the ability to set clear team goals that align with the broader objectives of the organization. When a team lacks focus or pursues goals that diverge from the company's vision, it can lead to underperformance, miscommunication, and wasted efforts. Aligning team goals with company objectives is not just a leadership strategy, it's a fundamental principle for fostering productivity, innovation, and long-term performance. In this chapter, we'll explore the importance of goal alignment, the challenges leaders face, and best practices for setting clear, achievable team goals.

The Leadership Struggles of Mark: A Cautionary Tale

Mark, a highly capable manager at a mid-sized technology firm, was promoted to lead a critical product development team during a period of rapid company growth. The leadership team was counting on him to bring innovative products to market. The pressure was immense, but Mark was confident in his ability to manage the team, having been a top performer in his previous roles.

However, over the next few months, cracks started to appear in his leadership approach. While Mark was excellent at providing technical guidance, his leadership approach had a major gap, he failed to create a cohesive vision for his team. He assumed that each team member understood the company's broader objectives and knew how their work fit into that vision. As a result, the team lacked clarity, and each member began pursuing different goals based on their individual perspectives. Without clear direction, projects were delayed, and the team's performance was increasingly out of sync with the company's overall objectives.

The disconnect became evident during a key product launch. While other departments had successfully aligned their deliverables to meet the company's strategic timeline, Mark's team was far behind. They had developed several innovative features, but most didn't align with the company's product roadmap. Senior leadership was disappointed, and Mark's reputation as a capable manager took a hit. His failure to establish and communicate clear team goals that aligned with company objectives led to inefficiencies and ultimately hurt the company's performance.

Mark's experience serves as a stark reminder that leaders must actively align team goals with organizational objectives. Without a clear strategy, even the most skilled teams can struggle to deliver meaningful results.

The Importance of Aligning Team Goals with Company Objectives

Aligning team goals with organizational objectives is essential for creating cohesion and maintaining focus within the company. When teams understand how their individual efforts contribute to the broader success of the company, they are more engaged, productive, and motivated.

Key Benefits of Goal Alignment:

- **Strategic Focus:** Directs the team's efforts toward core priorities, reducing wasted time on non-essential tasks.
- **Enhanced Collaboration:** Encourages cross-functional teamwork by helping departments understand how their roles intersect.
- **Increased Accountability:** Establishes clear expectations for team members, making it easier to track progress and performance.
- **Sustained High Performance:** Keeps teams focused on what matters most, ensuring long-term success and adaptability.

While aligning team goals with company objectives is crucial, it often comes with significant challenges for managers to implement effectively. One of the primary obstacles is a lack of clarity from leadership. When company objectives aren't communicated clearly to middle managers, it becomes difficult for them to align their team's efforts with the broader organizational vision. Another challenge is conflicting priorities, where teams may focus on department-specific goals that don't fully align with the company's strategic objectives, especially in larger organizations where departments operate in silos. In fast-paced industries, changing objectives create difficulties, as shifting company priorities can make it hard for managers to keep their teams' goals aligned. Lastly, resistance to change from team members who have grown accustomed to working autonomously can further complicate the process of alignment, as they may be hesitant to adjust their focus to meet new or evolving company goals.

To overcome these challenges, managers must communicate effectively, involve team members in the goal-setting process, and foster a culture of adaptability. Regular communication with senior leadership is critical to ensure that managers understand evolving objectives of the organization and can pivot their team's focus accordingly.

How to Set Achievable Goals & Effectively Communicate Them

The process of setting goals involves more than simply stating a target. It requires careful planning, communication, and active collaboration.

To ensure goals are both achievable and effective, leaders should follow a structured approach. First, applying the SMART framework to ensure goals are Specific, Measurable, Achievable, Relevant, and Time-bound. This method eliminates ambiguity and makes it easier to track progress. Collaborative goal-setting is also crucial—by involving team members in defining goals, you foster greater commitment and motivation. Additionally, it's important to align team goals with company objectives by regularly revisiting the organization's mission and asking how each team goal contributes to it. To make large goals more manageable, break them into manageable milestones that the team can accomplish step-by-step, reducing overwhelm. Finally, communicate regularly to keep goals top of mind. Use team meetings, one-on-one check-ins, and written documentation to consistently reinforce these objectives. By taking a thoughtful and structured approach, leaders create clarity, sustain focus, and drive measurable success within their teams.

Key Performance Indicators (KPIs): What Are They and Why Are They Important?

Key Performance Indicators (KPIs) are measurable values that demonstrate how effectively a team or organization is achieving its goals. KPIs help leaders gauge performance and track progress toward alignment with specific objectives.

KPIs are essential for several reasons. First, they offer clarity by providing clear, measurable standards for success, reducing ambiguity around expectations. They also promote accountability, enabling managers to track performance and hold team members responsible for their contributions. KPIs support data-driven decision making, offering insights that allow managers to make informed choices based on actual data rather than assumptions. Lastly, KPIs help improve focus, as teams can concentrate on key metrics that align with the company's goals, ensuring they prioritize tasks that have the most significant impact.

Objectives & Key Results (OKRs): What Are They and Why Are They Important?

Objectives and Key Results (OKRs) is a goal-setting framework designed to help teams align their efforts with the company's broader objectives.

OKRs are valuable for several reasons. First, they help teams maintain focus on the most critical objectives that drive success. By establishing clear priorities, OKRs ensure that team efforts are aligned with the organization's top goals, fostering a cohesive approach to achieving results. Additionally, OKRs provide flexibility, allowing teams to adapt as business conditions change, allowing teams to remain agile and responsive to new challenges. Finally, OKRs promote transparency within the organization, as everyone is aware of the priorities and can see how their contributions fit into the larger picture. This visibility enhances collaboration and commitment across teams.

In my last role, the company used OKRs for goal setting. It was my first experience utilizing OKRs to set my quarterly goals. It took me a minute to fully grasp the concept, but once I was able to create high impact OKRs, I could clearly see how my goals, and those of other departments, aligned with the goals of the organization. The transparency across departments was invaluable. To learn more about OKRs visit www.whatmatters.com for an in-depth understanding of how they can impact your organization, along with training and in-depth resources to get you started.

Best Practices for Implementing KPIs & OKRs

Implementing KPIs and OKRs requires thoughtful planning and consistent follow-through. Implementing best practices for setting and managing Key Performance Indicators (KPIs) and Objectives and Key Results (OKRs) is crucial for driving team success. First and foremost, setting clear expectations is the first step—every team member should fully understand what is being measured and why these metrics are important for the overall goals of the organization. This clarity fosters a shared understanding of priorities.

Using data to establish a baseline is also crucial when setting KPIs. By analyzing historical performance and relevant metrics, teams can define realistic targets that are both challenging and attainable. Regular reviews of KPIs and OKRs are also necessary to track progress and make adjustments as needed, ensuring the team remains agile and aligned with evolving business objectives. Encouraging team members to take ownership of their KPIs fosters a sense of responsibility, increasing motivation and commitment to achieving results. Lastly, finding the right technology to track KPIs and OKRs is a must. Several tools are available to help streamline tracking and reporting.

It is important to celebrate successes. Acknowledging and rewarding the team when they meet or exceed their KPIs not only reinforces positive behaviors, builds morale, and cultivates a culture of high performance within the organization. This combination of clear expectations, data-driven targets, ongoing reviews, individual ownership, and recognition creates a powerful framework for achieving organizational success.

Evaluating the Impact of Aligned Goals with Organization Objectives

Evaluating goal alignment is critical to ensuring that team efforts contribute to the broader success of the organization. Here are a few methods for you to stay on top of evaluating the impact your goals have had on your team and organization. Leaders should assess impact using a structured evaluation process that includes performance reviews, feedback loops, and outcome measurement.

Methods for Evaluation:

- **Performance Reviews:** Regularly assess team performance in relation to the company's objectives during team meetings. In addition, do not negate the importance of having 1-on-1 meetings with your team members. This provides another level of accountability for you and your team members.

- **Feedback Loops:** Create a feedback loop where team members, managers, and senior leadership can share insights on goal alignment. Town hall meetings are a great way for your team to share successes, losses, what was learned, and give an update on new KPIs and OKRs.

- **Outcome Measurements:** Look beyond task completion and measure the outcomes that were achieved. Did the team's work contribute meaningfully to the company's strategic goals? What could be done for the outcome to be completed? What additional resources are needed to get to the outcome?

- **Adjust As Needed:** Goal alignment is an ongoing process. If team goals are not contributing effectively to organizational objectives, it's essential to adjust them.

Seven Strategies for Defining Team Goals & Aligning Them with Organization's Strategy

Aligning team goals with broader company strategy creates a unified direction, fosters accountability, and enhances overall efficiency. Such alignment ensures that every team member understands their role in the larger mission, fostering a sense of purpose and accountability that drives performance. By establishing clear goals in harmony with the organization's strategy, leaders can more effectively monitor progress, adapt to changes, and cultivate a culture of collaboration that maximizes team potential.

1. **Know and Understand the Organization's Goals:** As a leader, you must have a deep understanding of the company's mission, vision, and strategic goals to set team objectives that directly contribute to long-term success.

2. **Develop Clear, Measurable Objectives for Your Team:** Your team's objectives should be specific and measurable. Use frameworks like KPIs and OKRs to ensure your goals are aligned with organizational priorities and can be evaluated over time. Leverage the right technology for tracking data.

3. **Involve Team Members in the Goal-Setting Process:** Engage your team in setting goals to encourage buy-in and commitment. When team members have a say in the process, they are more likely to be committed to achieving those goals.

4. **Foster Team Collaboration to Achieve the Big Picture:** Break down silos between teams and departments; encourage collaboration. Every team member should understand how their work contributes to the larger organizational objectives.

5. **Ensure Your Team Is Equipped with the Right Resources:** To achieve their goals, your team needs access to the necessary resources—whether it's training, technology, or additional personnel. Leaders should identify gaps and provide access to necessary resources.

6. **Don't Think It's Beneath You to Roll Up Your Sleeves:** As a leader, your support is crucial. Be willing to step in when needed and provide guidance and direct support to help your team meet their objectives.

7. **Consider Adding a Project Manager for Data Tracking & Outcomes:** If you are not technologically savvy or experienced in tracking data, I highly recommend you add a project manager who can. In addition, this person can be the point of contact for your team members and managers with data collection, reporting, and training on tracking tools. This will save you and your team lots of time and you will have access to the data you need!

 ## Dr. Rhonda's Leadership Lesson: Defining and Aligning Organizational and Team Objectives

The alignment of organizational and team objectives ensures that everyone is working toward common goals and moving in the same direction. This drives peak performance, fosters collaboration, and sustains high performance over time. Leaders who focus on goal alignment can ensure that their teams remain focused, motivated, and equipped to succeed.

By taking an active role in setting and communicating clear goals aligned with the organization's strategic objectives, leaders not only drive individual and team success but also contribute to the long-term success of the entire organization.

 ### Power Move

Download the ***Organization & Team Objectives Alignment*** worksheet at www.beinfluentialnow.com to ensure that your team's objectives are clearly aligned with the objectives of your organization. (Password : **BINow2025**) (Case Sensitive)

CHAPTER

08

THE ACCOUNTABILITY PLAYBOOK: CLARIFYING ROLES FOR PEAK PERFORMANCE

> You have to be proactive and hold team members accountable when it comes to ensuring that project outcomes meet your expectations.
>
> **DR. RHONDA L. ANDERSON**

When I started a new role, I quickly realized that while I had a fantastic manager, there was something missing—role clarity. My manager was supportive and approachable, but there were no clear boundaries or expectations for my position. I soon found myself in a dilemma. I loved the company and enjoyed working with my manager, but I felt lost without clear direction. I didn't have well-defined goals or projects, leaving me uncertain about how to measure my success. If I wanted to thrive, I knew I needed to take action.

I decided to initiate my own role clarity and accountability sessions. I outlined clear expectations for myself and discussed them with my manager. I identified the initial projects that would drive my success and defined how I would measure my progress. That simple exercise became one of the most valuable leadership lessons I've ever learned. While my manager provided incredible support, if I hadn't taken the initiative to set role clarity, I would have felt frustrated and disengaged. As I moved into leadership roles, I realized that creating role clarity from the start was critical to creating a culture of accountability from the start. If I wanted to produce exceptional outcomes as a leader, I needed to ensure my team had clarity on their roles and hold them accountable along the way.

This chapter explores why role clarity is essential for both leaders and employees, the impact it has on accountability, and practical strategies for ensuring your team thrives in these areas.

The Importance of Role Clarity & How it Impacts Accountability

Role clarity is one of the most fundamental, yet often overlooked, components of a successful team. When employees understand their roles clearly, they know what is expected of them and how their work contributes to the broader goals of the organization. Without this clarity, team members can become disengaged, confused, and less productive. Ambiguity in job roles not only hampers individual performance but also undermines team dynamics and accountability.

When employees don't know what their role entails or how they fit into the larger picture, it becomes nearly impossible for them to take ownership of their responsibilities. Accountability thrives when people understand what they are accountable for and why it matters. This makes role clarity the foundation for cultivating a culture of accountability. In a clear role structure, employees can be measured against well-defined outcomes and performance expectations, which encourages personal responsibility and initiative.

A lack of role clarity, on the other hand, leads to missed deadlines, incomplete tasks, and growing frustration within the team. When employees are unclear about their responsibilities, it can result in overlapping duties, or worse, tasks being left undone entirely. Without a clear understanding of roles, accountability breaks down, and leaders struggle to identify where things went wrong and addressing them effectively.

As a leader, ensuring that each team member knows their role and understands their deliverables is not just a one-time task, it requires ongoing communication and adjustment. When employees are given clarity about their role, they have a solid framework to build on, which fosters accountability and helps them contribute effectively to the team's success.

What is Accountability in Leadership? Why is it Important for Teams?

Accountability in leadership refers to the practice of holding both yourself and your team responsible for achieving agreed-upon goals and meeting performance standards. In an accountable team, leaders ensure that expectations are clear, responsibilities are distributed appropriately, and each team member understands their role in the process.

For teams, accountability means that each person is responsible for their own contributions while remaining committed to the team's collected success. It's the assurance that individuals will follow through on their commitments and that leaders will ensure their team members have the resources and support necessary to meet those commitments. Accountability is important for several reasons:

- ✦ **Creates a Culture of Ownership:** When employees know they are accountable for their actions, they take ownership of their tasks and outcomes. This drives engagement and motivation, as they see their efforts directly impacting the team's success.

- ✦ **Promotes Transparency:** Accountability builds trust within the team. When responsibilities and expectations are transparent, it becomes easier for teams to collaborate, share feedback, and address issues proactively.

- ✦ **Enhances Performance:** Accountability leads to higher performance. When employees are held responsible for their work, they are more likely to meet deadlines, adhere to quality standards, and continually strive for excellence.

- ✦ **Encourages Continuous Improvement:** Teams that embrace accountability are more likely to identify areas for improvement and take steps to enhance their processes and outcomes. It creates a mindset of being open to growth and constant development.

Without accountability, teams can easily become complacent, disengaged, and directionless. Leaders may struggle to drive the results needed to meet organizational goals. Cultivating accountability is essential for maintaining high standards, fostering innovation, and ensuring that teams perform at their best.

Benefits of Cultivating Accountability

Cultivating accountability in the workplace yields numerous benefits that enhance both individual and team performance, creating an environment where employees take ownership of their responsibilities and contribute to collective success. One of the most immediate outcomes is increased productivity, as employees who are held accountable for their tasks tend to be more focused and motivated, leading to more consistent and efficient output. Accountability also promotes open communication, fostering an environment where team members are comfortable seeking clarification and collaborating to solve problems. This clear line of communication reduces misunderstandings and helps teams stay aligned, ultimately boosting overall effectiveness.

In addition to improving communication, accountability strengthens relationships within the team. When everyone knows that their colleagues are responsible for their work, trust is built, creating a more cohesive and supportive team dynamic. This trust further enhances decision-making, as individuals feel empowered to contribute meaningful insights, knowing they are accountable for their input. As a result, teams make better, more informed decisions. Lastly, accountability drives higher employee engagement, as workers who feel responsible for their tasks develop a stronger connection to their roles and the team, leading to increased job satisfaction, long-term commitment, and improved retention.

By embedding accountability into the team culture, leaders can drive better outcomes, improve team dynamics, and create a more motivated and engaged workforce.

Accountability vs. Blame: Understanding the Difference

It's essential to distinguish between accountability and blame. In an accountable team, individuals take ownership for their actions and learn from mistakes. It's a positive force that encourages growth and resilience. Blame, on the other hand, is rooted in finding fault and assigning guilt. It's a destructive behavior that leads to an environment of fear, resentment, and disengagement that stifles both individual and team progress.

As a leader, fostering accountability means creating an environment where team members feel comfortable owning up to mistakes and using them as learning experiences. This approach builds trust and encourages individuals to feel supported rather than fearful of repercussions. Blame, however, erodes trust, discourages risk-taking, and damages team morale. Accountability is about holding people responsible in a way that is constructive, while blame is about pointing fingers and avoiding responsibility.

Model the Way: Don't Be Afraid of Rising to the Challenge of Enhancing Accountability

Leadership is not just about setting expectations; it's about modeling the behavior you want to see in your team. To cultivate accountability, leaders must first demonstrate it themselves. This means taking ownership of your own responsibilities, being transparent about your expectations, and holding yourself accountable for the team's success.

Leaders who model accountability are more likely to inspire the same behavior in their team. Don't be afraid to rise to the challenge of enhancing accountability within your team. It may require difficult conversations, regular follow-ups, and consistent effort, but the rewards are worth it. When accountability is a core value, teams perform at their best, trust is built, and the organization thrives.

Strategies for Ensuring Employees Have Role Clarity & Enhancing Accountability

Clear roles and strong accountability are the foundation of any high-performing team. Without clarity, employees become disengaged, tasks overlap, and accountability erodes. By setting clear expectations, promoting accountability, and regularly reevaluating roles and responsibilities, leaders can create an environment where teams thrive and deliver exceptional results.

Four Strategies for Strengthening Role Clarity

1. **Update Job Descriptions:** Ensure that every role on your team has an up-to-date job description that clearly outlines responsibilities, expectations, and key deliverables. This is a foundational step in providing role clarity.

2. **Reevaluate Responsibilities Regularly:** As business needs evolve, roles and responsibilities should be reevaluated. This helps ensure that employees' duties remain relevant and aligned with organizational goals.

3. **Create Standard Operating Procedures (SOPs):** SOPs and work processes should be established for each team or position. This provides a clear roadmap for employees to follow, reducing ambiguity and standardizing best practices around how tasks should be completed.

4. **Clarify Priorities for New Employees:** When onboarding new team members, take the time to clarify their role and immediate priorities. This sets the tone for their future performance and ensures they are set up for success from day one.

Six Strategies for Enhancing Accountability

1. **Make Accountability a Core Team Value:** Establish accountability as a non-negotiable cultural norm within your team. This sets the expectation that every team member is responsible for their own contributions and holds others accountable in a constructive way.

2. **Set Clear Expectations:** Be explicit about your expectations from each team member. Clear expectations provide a roadmap for success and give employees the clarity they need to take ownership of their performance.

3. **Lead by Example:** As a leader, you need to model accountability in your own actions. Be transparent, reliable, and consistent about your own responsibilities and follow through on your commitments. This sets the tone for the rest of the team.

4. **Encourage Open Communication:** Cultivate a space where open communication is encouraged. Empower team members to voice concerns, share updates, and solve problems collaboratively, without fear of repercussions. This fosters accountability and helps teams stay aligned.

5. **Promote Self-Management:** Encourage employees to take ownership of their own tasks and manage their workload independently. Empower them to set

personal benchmarks and take pride in their progress. This builds a sense of autonomy and accountability within the team.

6. **Prioritize 1:1 Meetings:** Regular one-on-one meetings with team members are essential for maintaining accountability. These meetings provide an opportunity to review progress, address challenges, and ensure that everyone is on track. These meetings offer support and guidance.

 ## Dr. Rhonda's Leadership Lesson: Continuous Evaluation of Roles and Accountability

One of the most valuable leadership lessons is the need for continuous evaluation of roles and processes to ensure they remain aligned with the evolving needs of both the team and the organization. To stay ahead, leaders must adopt a mindset of regularly reviewing roles and responsibilities on an annual basis, making necessary adjustments as team dynamics and business conditions shift.

Additionally, maintaining accountability within a team requires proactive effort. It's not enough to set expectations once and assume the team will follow through. Leaders must actively monitor progress, provide timely feedback, and make adjustments along the way. The phrase, "inspect what you expect," is especially relevant when cultivating accountability. Leaders must consistently check in with their teams, offer guidance, and hold them accountable for their progress to drive success.

Lastly, fostering accountability demands adaptability. As teams evolve and new challenges emerge, leaders must remain agile, continuously refining their approach to role clarity and accountability to ensure sustained team performance and engagement.

Power Move

First, select 3-5 strategies from the Strategies for Strengthening Role Clarity list above that you plan on implementing with your team. Then, follow the *Silver Hawk Coaching & Consulting* LinkedIn business page and send us a message sharing the strategies you've chosen! We will share them on our business page. Your strategies may help someone else!

Let's connect on LinkedIn (@DrRhondaAnderson), where I regularly share insights on leadership and talent development. Subscribe to our newsletter, *10X Your Talent*, for more strategies on leadership excellence!

IGNITE POTENTIAL: INSPIRING AND EMPOWERING YOUR TEAM TO EXCEL

> "
>
> Ignite the potential of your employees by empowering them to see beyond limits, motivating them to thrive and innovate with purpose.
>
> **DR. RHONDA L. ANDERSON**
>
> "

The Turning Point in Tracy's Leadership Journey

One of my past coaching clients, whom we will call Tracy, struggled with empowering her team. As a department head at a fast-growing tech company, she found herself at a critical juncture. She prided herself on being hands-on, immersed in every project her team tackled. Her motto was simple: "If you want something done right, you have to do it yourself." For a while, this strategy worked. Her department delivered exceptional results, and she earned a reputation of being a high performer. But as the company expanded, Tracy's workload grew exponentially. She found herself working late into the night, feeling constantly overwhelmed by the demands of her job. Meanwhile, her team, once eager and engaged, was slowly losing motivation. Their frustration with being sidelined was palpable.

Then came the breaking point. A critical project, one that had the potential to define the company's future, missed a major deadline. Tracy, in her effort to maintain control, had become a bottleneck. She simply couldn't keep up with the workload, and her reluctance to delegate cost her team the chance to shine. After the missed deadline, Tracy's boss intervened, seeing the exhaustion in her eyes and the frustration of her team. The advice was simple yet profound: "Delegate, trust your team."

Initially, Tracy resisted the idea. Delegating felt like relinquishing control, something that didn't sit well with her perfectionist tendencies. But with no other choice, she began to assign key tasks to her team members. What followed was nothing short of a revelation. Her team not only met the revised deadline, but they also exceeded expectations, offering creative solutions that Tracy had never considered. The department's productivity soared, and the team regained their enthusiasm and drive.

Tracy's transformation proved a powerful leadership lesson: Delegation wasn't about losing control; it was about empowering her team. By trusting them with responsibility, she gave them the autonomy to excel. This experience reshaped her leadership style, turning her into a more effective, trusted leader. Her team, now empowered, became more motivated, innovative, and engaged. Tracy's journey is a lesson for all leaders: when you delegate, you're not only lightening your own load, you're giving your team the chance to thrive.

Effective delegation allows leaders to harness the strengths of their team, motivating them by giving autonomy and fostering a sense of ownership, which ultimately drives better results for the entire organization.

Effective Delegation: Empowering Through Trust

Delegation is one of the most powerful tools in a leader's arsenal, yet many leaders struggle with it. A common misconception is that delegation equates to losing control and prevents them from tapping into the full potential of their teams. In reality, delegation is not about relinquishing responsibility, it's about distributing it wisely. It's about leveraging the unique strengths of your team members and giving them the opportunity to take ownership of their work.

Tracy's story demonstrates how delegation can transform a team's dynamic. By handing over key tasks to her team, Tracy was able to shift from a state of burnout to a position where her leadership was truly making an impact. Delegation requires trust—trust that your team can and will deliver. It also requires leaders to shift their focus from micromanaging every detail to guiding, supporting, and empowering their team.

When leaders delegate effectively, they allow their teams to grow in confidence, capability, and creativity. Delegation is not just about efficiency; it's a way to cultivate growth, autonomy, and innovation within your team. Each time a leader delegates, they are providing a development opportunity that will strengthen both the individual and the organization.

Effective delegation starts with a deep understanding of your team. By recognizing the strengths, skills, and potential of each team member, you can assign tasks that align with their abilities, setting them up for success. Clear expectations are crucial. Define what success looks like and communicate desired outcomes to ensure that everyone is on the same page. It's equally important to provide the necessary resources—whether it's tools, knowledge, or support—so that your team can complete the task without unnecessary roadblocks. Once you've empowered your team to take ownership, resist the urge to micromanage. Trust them to execute, but remain available for guidance if needed. Finally, delegation is not complete without reviewing the results and offering constructive feedback. This follow-up allows for continuous improvement and growth, ensuring that both the team and the leader evolve together.

The Autonomy Advantage: Why Great Leaders Let Go

Autonomy is a cornerstone of motivation and engagement. Research has shown that when employees are trusted to take initiative and make decisions, they are more motivated, productive, and satisfied with their work. Encouraging autonomy does not mean leaving your team to their own devices without guidance. Rather, it is about giving them the space to be creative, to take ownership of their responsibilities, and to make meaningful contributions.

Tracy learned that by encouraging autonomy, she was fostering a culture of trust and accountability. Her team members no longer felt like mere executors of her vision; they became active participants in shaping the success of their projects. When employees feel empowered to make decisions and contribute to the bigger picture, their sense of ownership increases. This, in turn, boosts motivation and leads to higher levels of engagement. When Tracy's team felt empowered to make decisions and contribute to the bigger picture, their motivation and engagement skyrocketed.

Fostering autonomy in your team begins with encouraging initiative. Give your team members the freedom to propose their own ideas and solutions, allowing them to take ownership of their contributions. Supporting creativity is equally essential—create a culture where experimentation and innovation are not just welcomed but celebrated. This opens the door for fresh perspectives and dynamic problem-solving. Flexibility plays a crucial role as well. By focusing on outcomes rather than rigid processes, you empower team members to approach tasks in a way that suits their strengths, promoting efficiency and personal growth. Finally, empower your team to tackle challenges head-on without immediate oversight. Trust them to navigate obstacles independently. Encouraging them to navigate without immediate oversight not only builds their confidence but also sharpens their problem-solving skills. Through these practices, you'll create a culture of autonomy where team members feel empowered, motivated, and accountable.

Motivating Team Members: Keeping the Fire Alive

Motivation is the fuel that drives team performance. As a leader, your role is not just to manage tasks but to inspire and energize your team. Motivation can take many forms, sometimes it's recognition and praise, other times it's the satisfaction that comes from overcoming a challenge or achieving a goal. The key is to understand what motivates each individual on your team and to create an environment that nurtures that motivation.

For Tracy, motivating her team came naturally once she began to delegate effectively and encourage autonomy. Her team members felt trusted and valued, which reignited their commitment to the organization's goals. Motivation is not just about providing rewards or incentives—it's about creating a sense of purpose. When team members feel that their contributions matter, they are more likely to stay engaged and committed.

How to Sustain Motivation in Your Team:

- ✦ **Recognize Achievements:** Employees love being recognized for their efforts. Celebrate wins—both big and small. Acknowledging accomplishments and celebrating victories reinforces a sense of progress and boosts morale.

- ✦ **Provide Purpose:** Help your team see how their efforts contribute to the larger goals of the organization, giving their work deeper meaning.

- ✦ **Offer Growth Opportunities:** Encourage continuous learning and actively provide targeted professional development opportunities. This motivates and empowers your team to sharpen their skills, perform at higher levels, and own their career trajectory.

- ✦ **Cultivate a Positive Work Culture:** Foster a positive environment, where collaboration and support are at the core of your team's interactions. This cultivates a sense of belonging and encourages teamwork.

- ✦ **Give Regular, Constructive Feedback:** Providing constructive and timely feedback is key to keeping team members aligned with goals while also helping them stay motivated and continuously improve.

Together, these strategies create a culture where motivation thrives, driving both individual and collective success.

Six Strategies for Empowering & Motivating Your Team to Success

Great leadership is a balancing act. It requires managing immediate tasks while simultaneously developing your team for the future. Effective delegation, encouragement of autonomy, and motivation are the foundations of a thriving team. Here are some actionable strategies that will help you empower and motivate your team to achieve success:

1. **Don't Be Afraid to Delegate:** Trust your team to handle important tasks. Letting go creates growth opportunities and allows you to focus on overarching organizational objectives and initiatives.

2. **Capitalize on Strengths:** Identify and capitalize on each team member's unique skills and talents. Utilize tools like the DISC assessment, Clifton StrengthsFinder, or other assessments to better evaluate the skills of your team.

3. **Encourage Initiative:** Give your team the freedom to be creative, solve problems, and take ownership of their work without micromanaging. Remember, this is a growth opportunity for your team members. I am not saying take a total hands-off approach but give them space to utilize their expertise.

4. **Empower Your Team:** Empowerment fuels motivation. When team members feel trusted, they become more engaged, committed, and less likely to leave your

team or the organization. If you are looking to increase your influence with your team members, this is a great way to achieve it!

5. **Avoid Micromanagement:** Trust your team to get the job done. Check in to support progress, not to control every detail. Micromanaging is one of the quickest ways to destroy the morale and productivity of your team.

6. **Set Clear Expectations:** Ensure that everyone understands their role, the task at hand, and the desired outcome. Provide support and training if necessary.

 ## Dr. Rhonda's Leadership Lesson:

Empowering and motivating your team is not just about delegating tasks or setting expectations, it's about creating an environment where your team can thrive. Effective delegation allows you to focus on high-level priorities while giving your team members opportunities to develop their skills. Encouraging autonomy fosters innovation and accountability, while motivation ensures that your team remains engaged and committed to their goals.

By implementing these strategies, you're not only enhancing your leadership skills but also giving your team the tools they need for career growth and success. It's a win-win. You'll have a team that is more productive, creative, and motivated, while you'll have more time to focus on strategic initiatives that drive the organization forward.

As a leader, your success is tied to the success of your team. When you empower your team, you create a ripple effect that drives performance, innovation, and engagement across the organization. Remember, great leaders don't just manage, they inspire, motivate, and empower those around them.

Power Move

Now that you've learned how to empower and motivate your team, I'd love to hear your thoughts! Follow our *Silver Hawk Coaching & Consulting* LinkedIn business page and send a message sharing the strategies you will use to empower and motivate your team! We will share them on our business page.

Also, don't forget to connect with me on LinkedIn (@DrRhondaAnderson), where I regularly share leadership insights and talent development strategies.

Subscribe to our newsletter, *10X Your Talent*, for powerful expert tips on leading high-performance teams that will propel your team forward. Let's continue this journey of growth and leadership together!

CHAPTER

10

THE INNOVATION EDGE: TALENT DEVELOPMENT AS A CATALYST FOR GROWTH

Strive to build a learning culture that provides opportunities for employees, from entry-level to the C-suite, to continuously enhance their expertise and talents.

DR. RHONDA L. ANDERSON

Building a Culture of Learning from the Ground Up

In a previous role, I had the privilege, and the challenge, of building a learning infrastructure from the ground up. It wasn't easy, but it was necessary. The organization had grown quickly, and it became evident that we needed to formalize our approach to learning and development. To kick off this transformation, I first needed to secure buy-in from upper management. Without their support, even the most impactful of our learning initiatives would struggle to take hold. Once that hurdle was cleared, I worked on creating a learning philosophy that aligned with our company's vision and values. This philosophy became the foundation upon which all future programs were built.

Next, we rolled out leadership and management development programs that weren't just check-the-box exercises. They were practical, focused on real-world skills, and tailored to our organizational needs. But we didn't stop at leadership. Learning became contagious across all levels of the organization. Professional development opportunities were made available for everyone, from entry-level employees to seasoned managers. As a result, the entire company felt the impact. Employee satisfaction surged, engagement soared, and productivity skyrocketed. Cross-departmental collaboration improved as employees gained a better understanding of how their work interconnected. This transformation underscored a critical lesson: leaders must value learning and prioritize talent development. Upper management must be as enthusiastic about learning as the employees themselves.

The experience taught me a valuable truth about talent development, its importance cannot be overstated. When leaders invest in the growth of their teams, they're investing in the future of their organization. But that investment must be strategic, intentional, and ingrained in the company's culture. And, most importantly, leadership must be fully committed to making talent development a priority, not an afterthought.

Nurturing Excellence:
Why Talent Development Matters

At its core, talent development is the intentional process of identifying, attracting, retaining, and developing the talent necessary to achieve an organization's goals. It is an ongoing process that ensures employees have the skills, knowledge, and capabilities they need to thrive in their roles today and in the future. Effective talent development programs don't just focus on immediate needs; they build a pipeline of talent that can adapt and evolve with the organization.

One of the key components of talent development is identifying potential. This involves more than just looking at an employee's current performance, it requires a forward-thinking approach to evaluate who has the capability and drive to take on more significant roles as the company grows. Once the right talent is identified, the next step is attracting and retaining them. This requires a commitment to providing growth opportunities, a positive work environment, and a clear career path. Finally, development must be continuous. Organizations must commit to enhancing employees' skills and capabilities through training, coaching, and mentorship.

Without a robust talent development strategy, organizations risk stagnation. Employees who don't see a path for growth will disengage, and companies that don't prioritize development will struggle to attract top talent. In today's competitive market, investing in talent development is crucial to preparing employees for today's challenges and it also equips them to lead the future success of the organization.

Having a Talent Development Strategy That Meets Both Company and Employee Needs

A successful talent development strategy must be designed to meet both the long-term needs of the company and support the aspirations of its employees. For organizations, this means creating a strategy that aligns with business goals and addresses skills gaps critical to future success. Whether it's preparing employees for leadership roles, expanding technical expertise, or enhancing soft skills like communication and teamwork, the development strategy should be comprehensive and future-focused.

For employees, an effective talent development strategy addresses their personal career goals and offers clear opportunities for growth. Employees want to feel valued and see a path forward within the organization. By creating programs that cater to both the company's needs and the personal aspirations of employees, organizations can foster a culture of loyalty and long-term commitment.

A successful talent development strategy is a win-win: it builds a stronger organization while empowering employees to reach their full potential.

View Talent Development as an Investment, Not an Expense

One of the biggest hurdles many organizations face is viewing talent development as an expense rather than an investment. In reality, the return on investment (ROI) for well-executed talent development programs can be substantial. Companies that prioritize learning and development are more likely to attract and retain top talent, retain high performers, and drive innovation. Moreover, these companies experience fewer skill gaps, reduced turnover, and greater employee engagement.

When leaders treat talent development as a cost to be minimized, they miss out on the long-term benefits, such as higher retention, greater innovation, and a stronger leadership pipeline. In contrast, when leaders view it as a strategic investment, they unlock the full potential of their workforce. Developing talent requires time, resources, and commitment, but the payoff, for both the organization and its people, is well worth the investment. First, I want you to assess the capacity of your human resources team. Ask yourself, does our current staff have the expertise and bandwidth to develop and execute an enterprise-wide talent development strategy? If not, then outsourcing may be necessary. Next, I challenge you to evaluate your budget line by line and identify opportunities to allocate funds for talent development initiatives. There is no budget too small, even a modest investment in employee growth can yield significant long-term benefits.

If you need assistance with developing or revamping a talent development infrastructure that fits the needs of your organization and employees, my team and I are here to support you! In addition, if you have a talent development infrastructure in place that needs to be revamped, we can help! With more than 20+ years of combined experience in the talent development arena, we specialize in helping organizations implement customized, high-impact strategies that drive engagement, retention, and business success. We would love to help your organization reap the benefits of implementing a solid strategy. Let's work together to build a future-ready workforce.

How Talent Development Drives Innovation

Innovation is the lifeblood of any organization that aims to remain competitive in an ever-evolving changing business landscape. Throughout my professional career, I have encountered countless leaders frustrated about their teams not being innovative. If there is no talent development strategy in place, then there is no innovation. Talent development plays a critical role in driving innovation by equipping employees with the skills, knowledge, and mindset needed to think creatively and solve complex problems. Through continuous learning, employees stay updated on the latest industry trends, technologies, and evolving methodologies, allowing them to bring fresh, innovative solutions to their roles.

Organizations that prioritize a culture of learning and encourage employees to take risks and explore new ideas are more likely to drive meaningful innovation. When employees feel supported in their development and have access to resources that fuel creativity, they are empowered to contribute new perspectives that can lead to breakthrough advancements.

In many ways, innovation is the natural outcome of a robust talent development strategy. As employees refine their skills, they become more confident in challenging the status quo and seeking out new opportunities for growth and improvement.

Sustainable Management & Leadership Development

Sustainable management and leadership development involves creating programs that are not only impactful in the short term but also built to last. For leadership and management development to be sustainable, it must cascade throughout the entire organization. Every level of management and non-management roles, from entry-level team members to senior executives, should have access to learning opportunities, and these programs should be designed to evolve alongside the organization's needs.

Leadership and management development should not be reserved for senior executives alone. By developing a pipeline of leaders across all levels of the organization, companies can ensure they have the talent necessary to meet future challenges. Sustainable leadership development also requires ongoing measurement and evaluation. By using tools such as 360-degree feedback, performance metrics, and leadership assessments, organizations can continuously refine their programs to ensure they are driving the desired outcomes.

Sustainable development programs are essential for ensuring that leadership skills are not only acquired but also applied and embedded into the culture of the organization. If you are unsure where to start, my team and I can assist you with developing impactful management and leadership development programs from idea to implementation. In my experience of developing managers and leaders, I feel that structuring management and leadership development in a six- to eight-month cohort format yields the highest return on investment. This format provides participants with the time and space needed for meaningful reflection, learning, and transformation, ensuring long-term success for both individuals and the organization as a whole.

Value Providing Continuous Learning for Your Team and Yourself

As leaders, one of the most important things we can do is model continuous learning for our teams. Leaders who prioritize their own development set an example for their employees and create a culture where learning is valued. Continuous learning is essential for staying competitive, both at an individual level and for the organization as a whole.

For leaders, the learning journey never ends. Whether it's staying updated on industry trends, enhancing leadership skills, or developing new capabilities, continuous learning ensures that leaders remain agile and equipped to navigate the complexities of today's business landscape. This practice should also be implemented for your team. I challenge you to set a learning requirement for your team. Have them dedicate one hour per week to learning and tracking progress. You can take it a step further by allowing them to teach the team what they have learned, if what they learned is beneficial for the entire team. This kills two birds with one stone. First, setting a structured learning goal for your team will be beneficial and enhance productivity, collaboration, and team morale, the benefits are endless. In addition, you are helping your employees improve their public speaking skills. Communication and presentation skills are valuable to their growth and development as they progress along their career journey.

Providing continuous learning opportunities for employees is equally important as a leader's own development. It keeps the workforce engaged, sharpens their skills, and fosters a culture of innovation. When employees see their leaders investing in their own growth and encouraging them to do the same, it creates a ripple effect that positively impacts the entire organization.

Seven Strategies for Driving Talent Development and Continuous Learning

To successfully implement a robust talent development strategy, here are several actionable steps leaders can take:

1. **Evaluate the Current State of Talent Development:** Assess where your organization and team currently stand in terms of talent development. Identify any strengths, gaps, and opportunities for growth.

2. **Secure Buy-In from Upper Management for Learning Initiatives:** Ensure the CEO and upper management prioritize talent development and are committed to integrating it into the company culture. A company-wide learning philosophy should be in place.

3. **Develop Learning and Development Expectations for Your Team:** Set clear expectations around learning and development. Consider creating a specific learning philosophy and learning goals for your team that aligns with the broader company vision.

4. **Build Leadership and Management Development Pipelines:** Establish annual development plans for both current and future leaders. Consider offering management development for new and seasoned managers as well. This ensures a steady pipeline of well-equipped talent ready to take on leadership roles.

5. **Partner with HR, Recruiting, and Talent Development Departments:** Collaborate with these departments to design future-focused staffing plans that align with long-term organizational growth and workforce planning strategies.

6. **Provide the Right Tools and Technology:** Foster an environment of continuous learning by ensuring the necessary tools, mentors, coaches, and career development paths are in place. Implement robust feedback mechanisms to guide growth.

7. **Design Talent Strategies for All Employees:** Tailor talent strategies that apply to employees at every level. This ensures that development opportunities are equitable and accessible to everyone. A well-rounded approach to professional growth empowers employees at every stage of their careers, driving engagement and long-term retention.

By implementing these strategies, organizations can build a learning culture that fuels continuous improvement, innovation, and long-term success.

 Dr. Rhonda's Leadership Lesson:

A robust talent development strategy that promotes continuous learning is the cornerstone of attracting and retaining top talent. When you offer these opportunities to your team, you're signaling that your organization is invested in their growth and development. In return, employees will stay committed not just to their roles, but to the success of the team and the organization as a whole.

Talent development isn't just about meeting immediate business needs, it's about creating a thriving workplace where employees feel valued, engaged, and motivated to bring their best every day. And that, ultimately, is the key to long-term organizational success.

 Power Move

Ready to elevate your team's performance and build a strong talent development infrastructure? Visit https://www.drrhondaanderson.com/book-online to schedule a complimentary strategy session. Let's discuss how we can implement a tailored solution to enhance leadership, motivation, and team growth in your organization!

THE FEEDBACK FORMULA: RECOGNIZING EFFORT, DRIVING RESULTS

> " No surprises...you should discuss performance with your team members throughout the year. Never pass on recognizing your employees on a job well done!
>
> **DR. RHONDA L. ANDERSON** "

Revamping Performance Feedback & Recognition

In a previous role, I was tasked with overhauling the performance feedback process across an organization of several hundred employees. The existing system was outdated, with feedback being limited to only once a year during the annual performance review. This system had become a mere formality. Employees felt blindsided by evaluations while managers dreaded the tedious task of filling out standardized forms that had little impact. The result was a disengaged workforce, uninspired managers, and a lack of clarity around employees' career trajectories.

One of the first changes I implemented was to introduce Individual Development Plans (IDPs) for every employee, managerial and non-managerial alike. These IDPs were designed to foster continuous dialogue between employees and their managers throughout the year, not just at year-end. The plans focused on short-term and long-term goals, enabling employees to chart their career paths while identifying training needs and performance objectives. This shift allowed employees to approach conversations about their future with confidence, without fear of unexpected criticism.

At the same time, we emphasized to leaders across the organization that feedback needed to be an ongoing dialogue, not a dreaded annual conversation. Managers were encouraged to discuss performance regularly, using the IDPs as a guide to assess progress and make adjustments. The IDPs not only alleviated the surprise factor during merit increases but also empowered employees by giving them a clear sense of ownership over their development.

The transformation was nothing short of remarkable. Employee engagement soared, productivity increased, and the organization saw a marked improvement in employee retention. Leaders became more attuned to the needs of their teams, and employees felt recognized, valued for their contributions, and more invested in their roles.

Feedback that Fuels: Elevating Performance with Insight

Performance feedback is one of the most powerful tools a leader has at their disposal. When used effectively, it can transform the dynamics of a team, enhance team performance, and foster a culture of growth and development. However, feedback must be meaningful to have a lasting impact.

Meaningful feedback goes beyond a checklist of tasks completed or goals met. It involves a deep understanding of an employee's strengths, areas for improvement, and aspirations. Leaders need to tailor their feedback to the individual, acknowledging their contributions while also providing constructive criticism where necessary.

Performance reviews, while often dreaded, are essential for maintaining transparency and accountability—but they should never be the only time feedback is given. A meaningful performance review is not just a critique of past performance; it is an opportunity to set future goals, align on expectations, and discuss career development. This is where Individual Development Plans (IDPs) come in, allowing both managers and employees to have a structured conversation to outline career aspirations, track progress, and identify skill development opportunities.

Leaders should never wait until the end of the year to give feedback. Real-time, ongoing feedback ensures that employees stay aligned with the organization's goals and have the opportunity to course-correct throughout the year. This also removes the anxiety and tension that can accompany year-end reviews, creating an atmosphere of trust and openness.

The Power of Coaching & Mentoring Your Team

Coaching and mentoring are two of the most powerful tools that elevate feedback beyond mere evaluations. A leader who actively coaches their team invests in their development, providing them with the tools they need to succeed, not just in their current roles but in future endeavors as well.

Coaching is about guiding your employees to discover solutions on their own, empowering them to take ownership of their work and decisions. It involves asking probing questions, offering guidance without micromanaging, and encouraging reflection on both successes and failures.

Mentoring, on the other hand, is more focused on long-term development. A mentor is someone who shares their experience, offers career advice, and helps employees navigate the complexities of professional growth. Leaders who take on the role of mentor signal to their teams that they are invested in their future, fostering a sense of loyalty and trust.

Both coaching and mentoring help to create a culture where feedback is viewed as an opportunity for growth, rather than a critique. When employees feel supported in their development, they are more likely to take risks, innovate, and push themselves to achieve greater results. If you are unsure about how to effectively coach and mentor your team, then training is necessary. My team and I can teach you and other managers on your team how to effectively coach and mentor staff members to ensure that you and your employees are getting the most out of feedback conversations. In addition, if you and your managers do not have time to devote to coaching and mentoring, my team and I can provide those customized coaching services as well.

Developing a Succession Plan & Continuously Grooming Future Leaders

One of the most overlooked aspects of talent management is effective succession planning. Far too often, organizations wait until a leader leaves or is promoted before they start thinking about who will step into their place. This reactive approach can leave teams in a state of uncertainty, can disrupt productivity, and place unnecessary strain on teams.

A proactive leader understands the importance of continuously grooming future leaders. This doesn't just mean training someone to fill your role in the future, it means developing a pipeline of talent across the organization, at every level. You have to be intentional about this. Succession planning has to become non-negotiable and be taken seriously by upper management.

The 9-box strategy is one of my favorite approaches to succession planning because it offers a clear, visual framework for assessing both the performance and potential of employees. This grid divides employees into nine categories based on their current performance and future growth potential, helping leaders identify high performers, future leaders, and those who may need additional support. The simplicity of the 9-box grid allows for a more structured and data-driven discussion about talent, while also helping to uncover hidden potential within the organization.

What makes this method so effective is its ability to provide leaders with a holistic view of their talent pool. By mapping employees across these nine categories, you can quickly identify those ready for leadership roles, those who need targeted development, and those who may not align with the company's long-term goals. The 9-box tool also encourages targeted development plans, ensuring that top talent is nurtured, underperformers are coached, and the organization has a pipeline of future leaders prepared for critical roles. It's a comprehensive and strategic way to ensure that succession planning is not just reactive but proactive, leading to long-term success. If you would like more information about the 9-box strategy, there are many industry professionals sharing insights on YouTube and you can also find books and website resources that provide deeper guidance.

Succession planning starts with identifying high-potential employees and giving them the opportunities necessary for leadership. This can be accomplished through targeted leadership development programs, stretch assignments, and cross-functional projects that expose employees to different areas of the organization.

By actively preparing the next generation of leaders, you ensure the long-term success of your team and organization. You also create a culture of upward mobility, where employees see a clear path to advancement and are motivated to stay and grow within the company.

Relevant KPIs for Measuring Team Performance

Key Performance Indicators (KPIs) are essential for measuring the effectiveness of your team and the impact of your leadership. Without data, it's impossible to know where improvements need to be made or what strategies are working.

Some relevant KPIs for team performance might include:

- **Employee Productivity:** Are team members meeting or exceeding their performance targets?

- **Employee Engagement:** How engaged and motivated are team members in their daily work?

- **Turnover Rate:** Are employees staying with the company long-term, or is there a high rate of attrition?

- **Project Completion Rates:** Are projects being completed on time and within budget?

- **Customer Satisfaction:** How satisfied are your clients or customers with the work produced by your team?

In addition to these traditional KPIs, it's important to look at qualitative data. Use surveys, 360-degree feedback, and regular check-ins to gather insights into team dynamics, collaboration, and overall morale. This type of feedback can provide a more nuanced view of performance and highlight areas for improvement that might not show up in quantitative data. Tracking KPIs effectively requires dedicated resources. Lastly, there are plenty of internet resources available to calculate and analyze the above mentioned KPIs. Again, I want to stress the importance of your team having a designated project manager to track this data if you do not have the support of your human resources department.

Employee Recognition:
What It Is and Why It's Important

Employee recognition is one of the most powerful tools a leader can use to boost morale, increase engagement, and improve performance. Recognition doesn't always have to come in the form of grand gestures—it's the small, consistent acts of appreciation that often have the biggest impact. I am always amazed at how leaders still fail to implement simple employee recognition programs that do not have a major impact on their budgets. As the old saying goes, it's the thought that counts the most!

When employees feel recognized for their efforts, they are more likely to go above and beyond in their work. Recognition also fosters a sense of belonging and loyalty, both of which are crucial for employee retention. Employees want to feel valued, and leaders who make a point to acknowledge their contributions create a positive, motivating work environment.

Check with your human resources department to see if there are any programs in place that you can leverage. If not, it's time to get creative on your own! There are many ways to recognize employees, ranging from low-cost to high-cost options—here are a few ideas to get you started:

- **Verbal Praise:** A simple "thank you" or acknowledgment of a job well done can go a long way in boosting morale. You can also buy a stack of company-branded "thank you" cards and write a personal note of appreciation. This is another low-cost way to say thanks and it also goes a long way when showing appreciation. Employees love when you take time to write a quick note. Most people save these notes for a life-time because it means so much!

- **Public Recognition:** Highlight an employee's achievements during team or company-wide meetings, town halls, or in all employee emails. You can also get creative with this! Add the announcement to the company newsletter, social media, bulletin boards, and on electronic displays throughout the company.

- **Monetary Rewards:** Cash is king! Offering bonuses, gift cards, or even a paid day off can be powerful motivators. I would take it one step further, if you have the budget, and take the employee out for lunch or dinner.

.⁺⁺ **Career Development Opportunities:** The gift of growth is definitely a gift that keeps on giving! Offer training programs, leadership workshops, conference opportunities, or mentorship programs to show employees you are invested in their future. Don't sleep on offering opportunities for career growth, like offering new job responsibilities or stretch assignments.

.⁺⁺ **Company-wide Recognition Programs:** Create a formal recognition program where employees can nominate their peers for awards. It can be done cost-effectively, but if you want to go all out, you can plan an annual recognition event to celebrate employee contributions in a major way.

Whatever recognition method you choose, it's important that it feels authentic and is aligned with the values of your organization. Remember, you are aiming for consistency! You can start small and grow into implementing an enterprise-wide employee recognition program!

Five Strategies & Tips for Effective Performance Feedback

Giving effective performance feedback requires thoughtfulness, preparation, and consistency. Here are some strategies to ensure that your feedback sessions are impactful:

1. **Respect Your Employee's Time:** Be prepared for the meeting and have specific examples to discuss. I highly recommend that you track all one-on-one meetings with your employees throughout the year. This will help you prepare for a productive meeting and eliminates surprises during performance reviews.

2. **Ensure Open Communication:** Create a safe space for employees to share their thoughts and concerns. Make sure your team feels comfortable discussing their performance and career journey with you. It starts with developing relationships.

3. **Discuss Constructive Feedback:** A wise manager told me that when having constructive feedback discussions, remember, "Clear is kind!" Don't shy away from difficult conversations, but watch your tone! See them as opportunities for growth. If you fear having difficult conversations, develop this skill by attending training or partnering with someone from your human resources department to assist you.

4. **Tailor Feedback to the Individual:** Feedback is not a cookie cutter process! Each employee is different, and your approach should reflect their unique personality and needs.

5. **Create an Action Plan:** End every feedback session with clear next steps and hold employees accountable for taking action throughout the year. I recommend implementing an Individual Development Plan (IDP) as a part of your feedback process.

Eight Strategies & Tips for Enhancing Employee Recognition

Implementing a successful employee recognition program doesn't have to be complicated or expensive. Here are some strategies to get you started:

1. **Check with HR:** Before launching your own program, ensure there isn't already a recognition program in place. If there is one in place, get a better understanding of it and see how you can collaborate with HR to make it work for your team.

2. **Identify Your "Why":** Take time to think through why you want to recognize your staff and what actions warrant recognition! Understand the purpose behind your recognition efforts.

3. **Determine Your Budget:** Whether you're working with a small or large budget, there are recognition options available. You do not have to spend a fortune. Start small and grow from there.

4. **Define Criteria & Share the Program:** Be clear about what behaviors or achievements will be recognized. Ensure recognition is fair and that the criteria is public and employees understand it. You don't want favoritism to ruin your recognition efforts. Make sure all employees are aware of how the program works.

5. **Appoint Champions:** Have managers lead by example in recognizing their teams. In addition, if you do not have capacity to lead the recognition efforts of your team, you can ask someone who is passionate about employee recognition to lead the effort.

6. **Keep it Simple:** Don't overcomplicate the process—focus on consistency and impact.

7. **Celebrate the Kickoff!:** Build excitement by making a big deal of the program's launch. Share it on social media, all employee emails, all employee events, and in every space, it can be announced.

8. **Measure Success:** Track the data! Regularly assess the effectiveness of your recognition program and make adjustments as needed.

Dr. Rhonda's Leadership Lesson:

Performance feedback and employee recognition should be an ongoing part of your leadership practice, not something that happens once a year. When feedback is given regularly, employees are more likely to stay on track with their goals. Recognition fosters a sense of belonging and motivation that drives engagement and productivity. As a leader, it's your responsibility to create an environment where your team feels supported, valued, and empowered to grow.

Remember, performance reviews and feedback conversations should not be met with anxiety or dread. They are opportunities for growth and alignment. By embracing performance feedback and recognition as integral parts of leadership, you'll create a more engaged, motivated, and high-performing team.

 ## Power Move

Never underestimate the power of recognition! Employees thrive when their efforts are acknowledged. Download the **Employee Recognition Strategy** worksheet at www.beinfluentialnow.com to create a simple, but highly effective plan to start recognizing your employees for a job well done. (Password: **BINow2025**) (Case Sensitive)

Need coaching or training for you and/or your team on how to give effective feedback, succession planning, or employee recognition? Schedule a 30-minute strategy session at https://www.drrhondaanderson.com/book-online.

CHAPTER

12

DATA-DRIVEN LEADERSHIP: HARNESSING ANALYTICS, AI, AND CONTINUOUS IMPROVEMENT

Fostering an environment of continuous improvement requires you to prioritize collecting data.

DR. RHONDA L. ANDERSON

The business landscape is evolving rapidly, and leaders who want to remain competitive and effective must move beyond relying solely on instinct and traditional methods. Data-driven decision-making, consistent process refinement, and leveraging technologies like Artificial Intelligence (AI) are no longer optional—they are essential tools for success. This chapter explores how leaders can foster a data-driven culture, embrace data-driven leadership, refine processes for innovation, and leverage AI to stay ahead of the competition.

The Cost of Ignoring Data

At a growing retail company, Karen (a past coaching client of mine), led a highly motivated sales team. Her primary goal was achieving monthly sales targets, and for a time, her team seemed to be thriving. Karen relied heavily on gut instinct and outdated strategies she had used for years, assuming that if sales were steady, everything was fine. Unfortunately, Karen failed to pay attention to past performance data, review customer feedback, or measure campaign effectiveness.

Sales eventually plateaued, but Karen brushed off the clear warning signs, attributing the stagnation to a typical slow season. Meanwhile, competitors were evolving—using data analytics to refine their approaches, predict market trends, and offer targeted promotions. By the time Karen realized something was wrong, several key clients had already left, and her team felt stuck using ineffective methods. When her boss intervened, it became clear that Karen's refusal to evaluate data had resulted in missed opportunities and stagnant growth. The company had to undergo a significant overhaul to catch up.

This story highlights an essential lesson: Leaders who neglect data and fail to evaluate outcomes limit their ability to refine processes, innovate and grow. Continuous evaluation fuels adaptation and improvement, keeping organizations competitive. Leaders like Karen fail not only their teams but also their businesses when they ignore the power of data.

The Data Advantage:
Transforming Culture Through Analytics

A data-driven culture encourages an organization to make decisions rooted in data insights, rather than relying on intuition alone. Organizations that champion data-driven strategies experience increased efficiency, improved decision-making, and heightened innovation.

Leaders who cultivate such a culture, empower their teams to make smarter decisions. Rather than relying on intuition or guesswork, teams can analyze historical data, market trends, and customer insights to guide their strategies. This approach allows leaders to predict outcomes with greater accuracy, enabling them to take calculated risks that drive better results. As a result, decisions on marketing campaigns, product development, and other critical areas are more likely to lead to higher success rates.

A culture centered on data also fosters accountability and transparency. When metrics and performance indicators are clearly defined and tracked, teams have a clearer understanding of what is working and where improvements are needed. Tracking and analyzing data also creates transparency between leaders and employees, as well as across departments, ensuring that everyone is aligned and focused on the same objectives. It also encourages a sense of responsibility, as team members can see how their contributions impact overall results.

Data-driven cultures promote continuous improvement by supporting regular evaluations of metrics and performance indicators. With a focus on refining operations based on real-time insights, organizations can stay agile and responsive in a fast-moving environment. Data reviews reveal inefficiencies and areas where optimization is needed, enabling leaders and their teams to implement changes that enhance performance and drive innovation over time.

Finally, leveraging data provides organizations with a distinct competitive advantage. Businesses that fail to embrace data risk falling behind competitors who use it to identify trends, optimize operations, and respond proactively to market changes. By utilizing data, organizations can anticipate shifts in the industry, remain adaptable, and seize opportunities ahead of the competition.

Embrace Data-Driven Leadership

Data-driven leadership is more than simply using data, it's about leading with a mindset that prioritizes evidence-based decision-making and empowers teams to integrate data in their day-to-day operations.

Data-driven leaders prioritize setting clear metrics and key performance indicators (KPIs) that align with organizational goals. These benchmarks provide a structured way to track progress, measure success, and pinpoint areas that require improvement. Without well-defined data points, leaders risk making decisions based on guesswork, rather than facts, which can lead to costly mistakes and missed opportunities for growth. Defining clear metrics ensures that decisions are grounded in objective insights rather than assumptions.

Informed business decisions rely on the analysis of relevant data, rather than relying solely on intuition or experience. Before launching a new product or entering a new market, leaders should carefully review customer data, sales trends, and competitor performance. This analytical approach allows leaders to predict outcomes more accurately, mitigating risks and guiding strategic decisions with greater confidence. By utilizing data, leaders make smarter choices that are aligned with both short-term goals and long-term vision.

Engaging teams in the data analysis process fosters collaboration and a deeper connection to organizational objectives. When leaders involve employees in evaluating data and decision-making, it empowers them to see how their work impacts the bigger picture. This approach not only improves alignment with the company's goals but also creates a culture of shared responsibility. Teams that understand how data informs strategy are more likely to contribute meaningful insights and take ownership of their roles.

One of the key challenges in adopting a data-driven approach is overcoming resistance to change. Employees may feel uneasy about moving away from familiar methods or may be intimidated by the complexity of data analysis tools. Leaders must create a supportive environment where data is made accessible and approachable. Offering training and resources to help employees confidently navigate data ensures that the entire team is equipped to embrace data-driven decision-making, a seamless and valuable part of the organization's culture.

Refining Processes and Driving Innovation

Data-driven organizations don't just stop at gathering data, they use it to refine processes and fuel innovation. In a world where efficiency and innovation are key to staying ahead, continuously evaluating and improving processes is essential for long-term success.

Regular data analysis allows leaders to identify inefficiencies in existing processes. Whether it's a production bottleneck or an underperforming marketing strategy, data reveals areas that need improvement. By addressing these inefficiencies, organizations can streamline operations, reduce costs, and enhance overall performance. This proactive approach ensures that businesses are constantly refining their processes and avoiding wasted resources.

As markets evolve, data enables leaders to adapt and stay competitive. Monitoring industry trends, customer behaviors, and market shifts provides valuable insights for refining strategies. For example, a retail company can analyze online shopping patterns to optimize its supply chain management or tailor marketing efforts to specific customer segments. This level of data-driven adaptability keeps organizations relevant and responsive to the changing business landscape.

Data also supports a culture of experimentation, which is essential for innovation. Leaders can use data to test new ideas, evaluate their effectiveness, and adjust their approach based on real-world outcomes. This approach reduces the risks associated with trial-and-error, making it easier to pursue innovative solutions while relying on evidence-based decision-making. As a result, organizations foster an environment where calculated risks are encouraged, leading to continuous improvement and growth.

Cultivating Innovation in the Age of AI

Artificial Intelligence (AI) is transforming the way businesses operate, offering powerful tools for data analysis, automation, and decision-making. Leaders who embrace AI can cultivate innovation, improve efficiency, and unlock new growth opportunities.

AI offers leaders powerful tools for solving complex problems by analyzing vast amounts of data and uncovering patterns that may go unnoticed by humans. From predicting market trends to optimizing supply chains and personalizing customer experiences, AI can provide creative solutions that keep organizations ahead of industry shifts and remain competitive. By integrating AI into problem-solving processes, leaders can continuously innovate and adapt to new challenges more efficiently.

However, while AI excels at data analysis and automating tasks, human creativity and intuition remain irreplaceable. Leaders must strike a balance between utilizing AI's strengths and fostering creativity within their teams. By allowing AI to handle repetitive tasks and large-scale data processing, employees can focus on more strategic initiatives, such as building relationships, thinking critically, and solving problems creatively. This balance ensures that technology enhances rather than replaces human ingenuity.

Implementing AI often requires collaboration across various departments, including IT, marketing, operations, and finance. Leaders need to assemble cross-functional teams that work together to integrate AI seamlessly into business processes. This collaboration demands clear communication, strong project management skills, and a shared vision of how AI can drive innovation. By guiding these teams effectively, leaders can harness the full potential of AI while fostering a culture of continuous innovation across the organization.

Six Strategies & Tips for Data-Driven Leadership and AI Integration

Leaders looking to implement a data-driven approach and integrate AI into their organization can follow these actionable strategies:

1. **Define Metrics that Align with Goals:** Identify key performance indicators (KPIs) that directly align with your organization's objectives. Whether it's sales growth, customer satisfaction, or employee retention, having clear metrics allows you to measure progress and make informed, data-driven decisions.

2. **Establish Data Collection Methods:** Establish how data will be collected, who will be responsible, and which tools or platforms will be used. Ensure your team has the tools and resources necessary to collect accurate and reliable data, whether through customer surveys, sales reports, or AI-powered analytics platforms.

3. **Analyze Data with Your Team:** Once you have collected the data, engage your team in the analysis process. Hold regular data-driven review meetings where you discuss insights, identify trends, and brainstorm potential improvements or strategies.

4. **Consistently Monitor and Refine Processes:** Data collection and analysis isn't a one-time effort—it requires consistent monitoring. Set up a system to regularly track key metrics, adjusting strategies and refining processes based on real-time insights. Continuous improvement is essential to maintaining a competitive edge.

5. **Use AI to Automate Routine Tasks:** AI can streamline workflows by automating routine tasks such as data entry, customer service inquiries, and inventory management. This frees up your team to focus on high-value initiatives like strategic planning and innovation.

6. **Leverage AI for Predictive Analytics:** Predictive analytics, powered by AI, helps leaders anticipate market trends, customer behaviors, and potential risks. Use AI-driven insights to make proactive, data-driven decisions that will give your organization a competitive edge.

Dr. Rhonda's Leadership Lesson:

As a leader, your ability to collect, analyze, and act on data is crucial for making high-impact decisions. In today's business landscape, success depends on embracing data-driven leadership and leveraging AI to refine processes and innovate continuously. The tough decisions you make today, based on data and outcomes, will pave the way for your organization's sustainability and long-term success. Don't be afraid to step out of your comfort zone and prioritize the collection and analysis of data. The rewards far outweigh the risks, and both your team and organization will thank you for it.

 ## Power Move

Now that you have learned the importance of data-driven leadership, share three key takeaways from this chapter. Email us at info@drrhondaanderson.com. Let's connect on LinkedIn (@DrRhondaAnderson), where I regularly share insights on leadership and talent development. Don't forget to subscribe to our newsletter, **10X Your Talent,** for powerful strategies to propel your team forward.

CHAPTER

13

PILLARS OF EXCELLENCE: CREATING A LEGACY OF HIGH-PERFORMANCE CULTURE

Listen, it is your responsibility as a leader to hold yourself accountable for fostering a culture of excellence and achieving high-impact results with your team.

DR. RHONDA L. ANDERSON

Cultivating a culture of excellence is more than a leadership mandate, it is a strategic imperative that lays the foundation for sustained organizational success. This chapter explores the transformative power of fostering a high-performing team, provides actionable strategies to achieve this goal, and highlights the necessity of adaptability, innovation, and continuous learning to stay competitive in an ever-changing landscape.

The Power of a Culture Shift: James' Story

At a mid-sized marketing firm, James managed a team that operated under a "good enough" mindset. Deliverables met the bare minimum requirements, innovation was scarce, and training opportunities were almost nonexistent. Feedback came only when mistakes were made, creating an atmosphere of criticism rather than encouragement. Over time, the team began to stagnate. Projects were increasingly delayed, quality declined, and once-loyal clients began to take their business elsewhere.

The breaking point came when the firm lost a key account to a competitor. During the exit interview, the client remarked that James' team lacked creativity and growth compared to their new partner, who fostered continuous learning and upheld high standards.

Shaken by this revelation, James realized that he had inadvertently cultivated a culture of mediocrity. He embarked on a mission to shift his leadership approach to rebuild his team's ethos by prioritizing professional development. He encouraged team members to acquire new skills, rewarded innovation, and established regular feedback loops that celebrated progress. Within a year, his team regained its edge, secured new accounts, and outperformed competitors in both creativity and results.

James' story underscores a critical truth: Leaders who fail to nurture excellence inadvertently create disengaged teams and lose opportunities. A culture of continuous development and high standards fuels innovation, drives growth, and ensures long-term success.

The Importance of Cultivating a Culture of Excellence

Excellence is not accidental; it is a deliberate pursuit that requires unwavering commitment. Leaders who embrace this mindset inspire their teams to achieve high-impact results. Expecting excellence doesn't mean being unreasonably demanding; it means fostering an environment where accountability, growth, and ambition thrive.

A culture of excellence links directly to measurable outcomes such as increased productivity, enhanced employee satisfaction, and improved client retention. Leaders must embody the standards they set, holding themselves and their teams accountable to these ideals. When leaders compromise on accountability or accept mediocrity, they inadvertently signal that excellence is optional, opening the door to stagnation, disengagement, and ultimately decline.

Continuous Learning: The Cornerstone of Excellence

Continuous learning is the lifeblood of a culture of excellence. Teams that prioritize learning stay ahead of industry trends, solve problems more creatively, and adapt to change with confidence. When continuous learning is not a priority, organizations shift from thriving to merely surviving. I am challenging you to assess your organization's learning function and make adjustments to strengthen it. Companies can implement a learning infrastructure for every budget. Be intentional about finding the money to invest in your team's growth.

Aligning professional development with company values reinforces organizational identity. For example, a company that values innovation should invest in training programs that enhance creative thinking. Similarly, leaders can use mentoring and coaching to help employees align personal growth with organizational goals.

When employees see that their development is prioritized, they become more engaged, motivated, and committed to the organization's success.

Change Management 101: Leading with Resilience

Change is an inevitable part of organizational growth and evolution. However, the success of any change initiative depends largely on how effectively leaders guide their teams through the process. Poorly managed change can result in confusion, resistance, and setbacks, while skillful change management can propel organizations toward greater resilience and adaptability. To navigate these transitions successfully, leaders must focus on three foundational elements: clarity, communication, and resilience.

Clarity is the starting point for effective change management. Leaders must clearly articulate the "why" behind the change, ensuring that team members understand its purpose and alignment with organizational goals and values. When employees see how a change connects to the bigger picture, whether it's enhancing customer satisfaction, improving operational efficiency, or staying competitive, they are more likely to support it. Leaders should take the time to address potential concerns and provide a roadmap that outlines the key steps and expected outcomes of the change initiative. This level of transparency helps reduce uncertainty and fosters a sense of shared purpose, making it easier for teams to align with the change.

Communication is equally critical during periods of transition. Transparent, consistent communication helps bridge gaps in understanding and mitigates fears or misconceptions that may arise. Leaders should establish open channels for dialogue, encouraging team members to ask questions, express concerns, and provide feedback. Regular updates on progress, challenges, and successes ensure that everyone feels informed and included in the process. When leaders communicate effectively, they build trust and create a culture of collaboration that makes transitions smoother and more productive.

Resilience is the third pillar of successful change management. Leaders must model adaptability and perseverance, demonstrating that they can remain focused and composed even in uncertain times. By exhibiting a positive attitude and a problem-solving mindset, leaders inspire their teams to approach change with confidence rather than fear. Resilience also involves learning from setbacks, recognizing that challenges are a natural part of transformation. This approach not only builds individual and team resilience but also strengthens the organization's ability to adapt to future changes.

Strategic change management, built on the principles of clarity, communication, and resilience, ensures that initiatives are executed effectively and with minimal disruption. More importantly, it positions the organization to thrive in an environment of constant volatility. Leaders who master these skills not only guide their teams successfully through change but also foster a culture of adaptability that becomes a competitive advantage in today's dynamic business landscape.

Innovation and Adaptability: Thriving in a Dynamic Landscape

Innovation is the heartbeat of excellence and a critical driver of success in today's fast-paced, ever-changing business environment. For organizations to thrive, leaders must intentionally cultivate a culture that embraces curiosity, encourages calculated risk-taking, and views failure as an essential part of growth. Without innovation, even the most successful teams risk stagnation and becoming obsolete in the face of rapid industry changes. Leaders who prioritize creativity, adaptability, and resilience unlock their team's full potential, ensuring long-term competitiveness.

Encouraging creativity is the foundation of fostering innovation. Leaders must create an environment where team members feel psychologically safe to share their ideas, even if those ideas seem unconventional or unrefined. Psychological safety allows individuals to contribute without fear of judgment or rejection, which in turn sparks collaboration and collective problem-solving. Regular brainstorming sessions, open forums for discussion, and dedicated innovation initiatives can empower teams to think outside the box. By showing genuine enthusiasm for diverse perspectives, leaders signal that creativity is valued and rewarded.

Promoting calculated risk-taking is another vital aspect in building a culture of innovation. Many teams hesitate to take risks due to fear of failure or negative consequences. Leaders must actively dismantle this mindset by celebrating experimentation and viewing setbacks as learning opportunities rather than liabilities. When leaders publicly acknowledge and appreciate well-thought-out risks, even those that don't succeed, they encourage their teams to step out of their comfort zones. This approach nurtures resilience and cultivates a growth mindset, where challenges and failures are stepping stones to greater achievements.

Staying adaptable and informed about industry changes is equally essential. Leaders should remain vigilant about emerging trends, technologies, and market demands, ensuring that their teams are equipped to pivot when necessary. This involves a commitment to ongoing professional development, strategic planning, and open dialogue about potential shifts in direction. Adaptable teams are better positioned to navigate uncertainty, seize new opportunities, and stay ahead of competitors. Encouraging innovation also means providing the right tools and resources to enable teams to turn creative ideas into actionable solutions effectively.

When teams embrace adaptability and innovation, they become agile and future-ready, capable of responding to industry shifts with confidence and ingenuity. Leaders who champion these values not only elevate their team's performance but also position their organization to maintain a competitive edge in an increasingly dynamic market. By embedding innovation into the organizational culture, leaders lay the groundwork for sustained excellence and enduring success.

Future-Proofing Your Leadership: Continuous Adaptation

Excellence in leadership is not a destination but a continuous journey that demands a deep commitment to lifelong learning and self-improvement. The rapidly evolving landscape of industries and organizations requires leaders to be proactive, adaptable, and resilient. A key strategy for achieving this is developing a personal learning ecosystem—a tailored framework that helps you stay informed, enhance your skills, and prepare for future challenges. This ecosystem should be dynamic, evolving alongside your career and the demands of your field.

One of the cornerstones of this ecosystem is the ability to anticipate future challenges. Leaders must stay informed about emerging industry trends, technological advancements, and potential disruptions that could impact their organizations. This forward-thinking approach allows you to identify opportunities for growth and innovation while leading with confidence. Whether through professional networks, industry publications, or conferences, staying ahead of the curve positions you as a strategic and forward-thinking leader.

Another vital component of your personal learning ecosystem is creating an influential leadership action plan. This plan should clearly outline your leadership vision, articulate your long-term goals, and provide a roadmap for achieving them. Setting measurable milestones and regularly reviewing your progress ensures you remain aligned with your objectives and adaptable to changes. A well-crafted action plan not only guides your leadership journey but also reinforces your commitment to excellence.

Investing in your development is perhaps the most impactful way to future-proof your leadership. Actively seek out coaching opportunities, attend workshops and seminars, and read to expand your knowledge base. Learning from experts and engaging with diverse perspectives enriches your understanding and equips you with innovative approaches to complex challenges. This commitment to growth enhances your capabilities and also inspires your team to pursue their own development.

By consistently prioritizing learning and adaptation, you position yourself as a resilient and future-ready leader. In doing so, you are able to navigate the complexities of today's business world with confidence and build a legacy of excellence that empowers your team and drives your organization toward long-term success.

Six Actionable Strategies for Cultivating Excellence

1. **Align Your Leadership Decisions with Company Values**: Ensure every decision you make and action you take reflects the organization's core values. Take time to think through your options. Before making key choices, revisit your company's core values.

2. **Create a Positive Environment**: Foster an atmosphere of collaboration, trust, and mutual respect. Be intentional about building positive relationships within your team.

3. **Set High Standards:** Never settle for mediocrity. Excellence should be the standard, not the exception. Take time to think about your department(s) and define what excellence looks like for each department. This makes a great team-building activity.

4. **Hire for Excellence:** Commit to hiring top talent. Bring in individuals who not only possess exceptional skills but also demonstrate a commitment to growth.

5. **Encourage Innovation:** Support creative thinking and calculated risks. Remember, if ideas fail, it is a learning experience.

6. **Leverage Earlier Strategies Shared:** Build upon the foundational leadership principles shared throughout this book.

**Dr. Rhonda's Leadership Lesson:
The Ripple Effect of Excellence**

Making a conscious effort to cultivate a culture of excellence positively impacts every aspect of your organization. Employee satisfaction and retention soar when individuals feel valued and empowered. Clients notice the difference, gravitating toward businesses that consistently exceed expectations.

As a leader, your commitment to high standards inspires those around you. Excellence is contagious. When modeled by upper leadership, it becomes ingrained in the organizational culture, driving long-term success.

 Power Move

Follow our *Silver Hawk Coaching & Consulting* LinkedIn business page and send a message sharing what you plan to implement to cultivate a culture of excellence. We will feature select strategies on our page. Subscribe to our newsletter, *10X Your Talent*, for actionable leadership strategies that will propel your team forward.

Let's connect on LinkedIn (@DrRhondaAnderson) or visit my website to schedule a complimentary 30-minute strategy session to elevate your leadership to the next level.

We want to hear from you! If you loved reading *The Influential Leader Blueprint*, please share your testimonial with us. You can email our team at info@drrhondaanderson.com. We would appreciate it!

EPILOGUE

Congratulations, you have reached the end of this book! You are now equipped with new strategies to help you elevate your leadership game and become the influential leader you are called to be. You are ready to take control of your leadership journey and lead with greater impact on a personal and professional level.

Keep this book within reach! It was written to be a blueprint for you to refer to whenever you need it. Don't feel overwhelmed with trying to implement all of the strategies at once. Take your time, but also take continuous, imperfect action. Implementing a few strategies at a time equates to major progress. Focus on getting 1% better each day!

The summary below highlights the key concepts explored in this book, designed to guide you on your journey to becoming an influential leader:

Chapter 1: Soaring with Purpose: Unlocking the Potential of Transformative Leadership

Discover how to lead with clarity, vision, and purpose, inspiring your team to reach extraordinary heights.

Chapter 2: The Mirror Within: Mastering Self-Awareness and Emotional Intelligence

Learn to cultivate deep self-awareness and emotional intelligence, the foundational skills of resilient and adaptive leaders.

Chapter 3: Values in Action: Defining Your Leadership Compass and Goals

Define your core leadership values and personal goals to create a compelling blueprint for authentic and impactful leadership.

Chapter 4: The Trust Equation: Building Unshakable Leadership Foundations

Master the art of building trust as the bedrock of effective leadership and cohesive team dynamics.

Chapter 5: The Art of Influence: Communication Tactics That Transform Teams

Transform your communication strategies to inspire action, foster alignment, and strengthen relationships.

Chapter 6: The Safety Net: Nurturing Psychological Safety and Team Belonging

Create a culture where psychological safety empowers individuals to contribute boldly and innovate freely.

Chapter 7: Aligned for Impact: Bridging Team Goals with Visionary Objectives

Develop the skills to align team objectives with organizational vision, driving unity and measurable outcomes.

Chapter 8: The Accountability Playbook: Clarifying Roles for Peak Performance

Clarify roles, set expectations, and cultivate a culture of accountability that propels your team to success.

Chapter 9: Ignite Potential: Inspiring and Empowering Your Team to Excel

Unleash the hidden potential of your team through empowerment, motivation, and strategic support.

Chapter 10: The Innovation Edge: Talent Development as a Catalyst for Growth

Leverage talent development and a growth mindset to drive innovation and foster a culture of continuous learning.

Chapter 11: The Feedback Formula: Recognizing Effort, Driving Results

Master the science of giving constructive feedback and recognizing achievements to boost engagement and performance.

Chapter 12: Data-Driven Leadership: Harnessing Analytics, AI, and Continuous Improvement

Learn to harness the power of data, AI, and agile processes to refine strategies and achieve breakthrough results.

Chapter 13: Pillars of Excellence: Creating a Legacy of High-Performance Culture

Discover the principles of building and sustaining a high-performance culture that stands the test of time.

The time is now! Take the strategies from this book, implement and execute them, and soar to greater heights as a leader. Remember, the leadership journey is not about you, it is about how you impact and lead within your sphere of influence and beyond. I am challenging you to choose to be GREAT! Choose to be INFLUENTIAL!

MEET DR. RHONDA ANDERSON

Meet Dr. Rhonda Anderson, Ph.D., CPC – Transformative Leadership & Talent Development Expert

Dr. Rhonda Anderson is a leadership strategist, Certified Professional Coach, Certified DISC Facilitator, and author of the empowering playbook for success, *The Goal Digger's Playbook: Eight Strategies for #NextLevel Success*. She is also the co-author of *The Quick and Dirty Guide to Entrepreneurship*, a modern guide for 21st-century startups. As the Principal and Chief Talent Development Officer at Silver Hawk Coaching & Consulting, Dr. Rhonda has become a driving force behind the success of forward-thinking organizations and leaders committed to growth, innovation, and transformation.

Based in the thriving metropolitan Atlanta area, widely recognized as the "Silicon Peach" and "Hollywood of the South", Dr. Rhonda's expertise spans over 15 years of experience in talent development, higher education, and consulting. She is recognized for her work in designing and implementing enterprise-wide learning infrastructures, leadership and management development programs, and talent management strategies that revolutionize organizational effectiveness.

A dynamic and sought-after public speaker, Dr. Rhonda captivates audiences with her engaging, relatable style and transformative insights. Her content challenges the status quo, equipping leaders with the tools to enhance performance, foster collaboration, and cultivate a thriving, inclusive workplace. Whether speaking on stage or in the boardroom, Dr. Rhonda empowers individuals and organizations to achieve next-level success.

Dr. Rhonda holds a Ph.D. in Higher Education Leadership from Mercer University. In addition, she has a Master of Human Resources Management degree from Keller Graduate School of Management. As the first person in her immediate family to earn advanced degrees, the achievement holds deep significance for Dr. Rhonda. Her ultimate goal has always been to pave the way for others in her family, inspiring them to dream bigger and become more than they ever thought possible.

Residing in metro Atlanta, Dr. Rhonda is married to James Anderson, and together they have raised three adult sons. Dr. Rhonda loves to spend quality time with her family and friends, travel the world, and indulge in self-care.

Book Dr. Rhonda Anderson to Inspire, Empower, and Transform Your Audience

Looking for a dynamic speaker who captivates audiences and delivers actionable insights? Dr. Rhonda Anderson is an award-winning Certified Professional Coach and seasoned talent development expert with over 15 years of experience. Known for her engaging and relatable style, Dr. Rhonda delivers powerful content on leadership, team dynamics, and organizational performance to every event.

Whether you're hosting a conference, corporate retreat, training session, or webinar, Dr. Rhonda delivers customized presentations tailored to your audience's unique needs. Her expertise in leadership development, emotional intelligence, and building cohesive teams equips participants with actionable tools to drive success and elevate their impact.

Elevate your event with a speaker who leaves a lasting impression. Book Dr. Rhonda Anderson today for an unforgettable experience that empowers your audience to lead with confidence, resilience, and purpose.

You can connect with Dr. Rhonda Anderson by visiting www.drrhondaanderson.com to inquire about collaborations and professional engagements.

Silver Hawk Coaching & Consulting

At Silver Hawk Coaching & Consulting, we specialize in empowering businesses to achieve exceptional results through innovative talent development strategies. Our approach blends deep industry expertise with a passion for leadership excellence. We provide comprehensive services, including the creation and launch of tailored leadership and management development programs, ensuring our clients' teams are equipped to excel.

With over 15 years of experience, Dr. Rhonda Anderson, Principal and Chief Talent Development Officer, and her team possess deep industry knowledge in designing and implementing robust talent development programs, leadership development, management development, and executive coaching. At Silver Hawk, we believe that strong leaders are the cornerstone of successful organizations, and we strive to cultivate this strength in every client we serve. Our solutions are designed to drive peak performance, align organizational objectives, and inspire continuous growth. We collaborate with organizations to unlock the full potential of their teams and propel them toward new heights. The success of our clients is our mission. Learn more at www.drrhondaanderson.com or connect with Dr. Rhonda at info@drrhondaanderson.com to continue the conversation.

Services Offered:

.⁺⁺ **Fractional Talent Development Leadership**: Transform your organization's leadership and talent capabilities by leveraging 15+ years of expertise. We provide strategic insight combined with hands-on coaching to elevate your team's performance and drive sustainable growth.

.⁺⁺ **Learning and Development Infrastructure**: Build a structured learning framework that fosters continuous growth and aligns seamlessly with your organization's mission, vision, and values.

- **Leadership Development**: Equip your leaders with the essential skills needed to inspire, motivate, and guide their teams to achieve outstanding results.

- **Management Development**: Empower your managers with practical tools and techniques to excel in performance management, conflict resolution, and team-building techniques.

- **DISC Facilitation**: Improve team dynamics and communication with certified DISC assessments, enabling your team to harness the strengths of diverse personality types for more effective collaboration.

- **Essential Professional Development Skills**: Accelerate your team's growth with a custom learning and development strategy designed to match your unique needs. Develop core competencies such as communication, time management, critical thinking, emotional intelligence, and psychological safety to drive team success.

- **Executive Coaching**: Elevate your leaders to their highest potential through personalized coaching designed to drive innovation and cultivate a culture of excellence.

How To Work with Dr. Rhonda Anderson

For more information on how to work with Dr. Rhonda and the services offered, visit www.drrhondaanderson.com or send an email to info@drrhondaanderson.com.

I. Complimentary Resources

- Connect with Dr. Rhonda on LinkedIn @DrRhondaAnderson for insightful tips and leadership strategies.

- Follow the Silver Hawk Coaching & Consulting LinkedIn business page.

- Subscribe to the "10X Your Talent" LinkedIn newsletter for additional action-oriented strategies to boost team performance and elevate your organization to new heights.

- Be on the lookout for free webinars and the launch of Dr. Rhonda's podcast.

II. The Influential Leaders Alliance: A Leadership & Career Development Community

✦ The Influential Leaders Alliance is a membership community that helps experienced leaders, emerging leaders, and entrepreneurs looking to strengthen their leadership and management skills to drive peak performance and build lasting confidence in the workplace. We empower members to define ambitious career goals and establish effective work habits that lead to transformative impact.

✦ When you join the community, you have access to exclusive 1:1 coaching, high-impact group coaching, monthly learning tracks, a resource library, powerful peer networking connections, and so much more—all focused on achieving peak performance and long-term career success.

Learn more about The Influential Leaders Alliance and the investment: https://influential-leaders-alliance.mn.co

III. Next Level Success Academy: The A.S.C.E.N.D. Leadership Development Coaching Program

A.S.C.E.N.D. is a comprehensive 6-step framework designed to empower leaders with skills to elevate their leadership, inspire their teams to achieve peak performance, and deliver extraordinary results.

This 6-month coaching program accompanies this book and can be conducted in cohorts or in a 1:1 format. An image of the framework is available on the next page.

Follow Dr. Rhonda to stay in the know for program updates and when it will be offered.

IV. Silver Hawk Coaching & Consulting

For a full list of services offered visit the *Silver Hawk Coaching & Consulting* section of this book or visit www.drrhondaanderson.com.

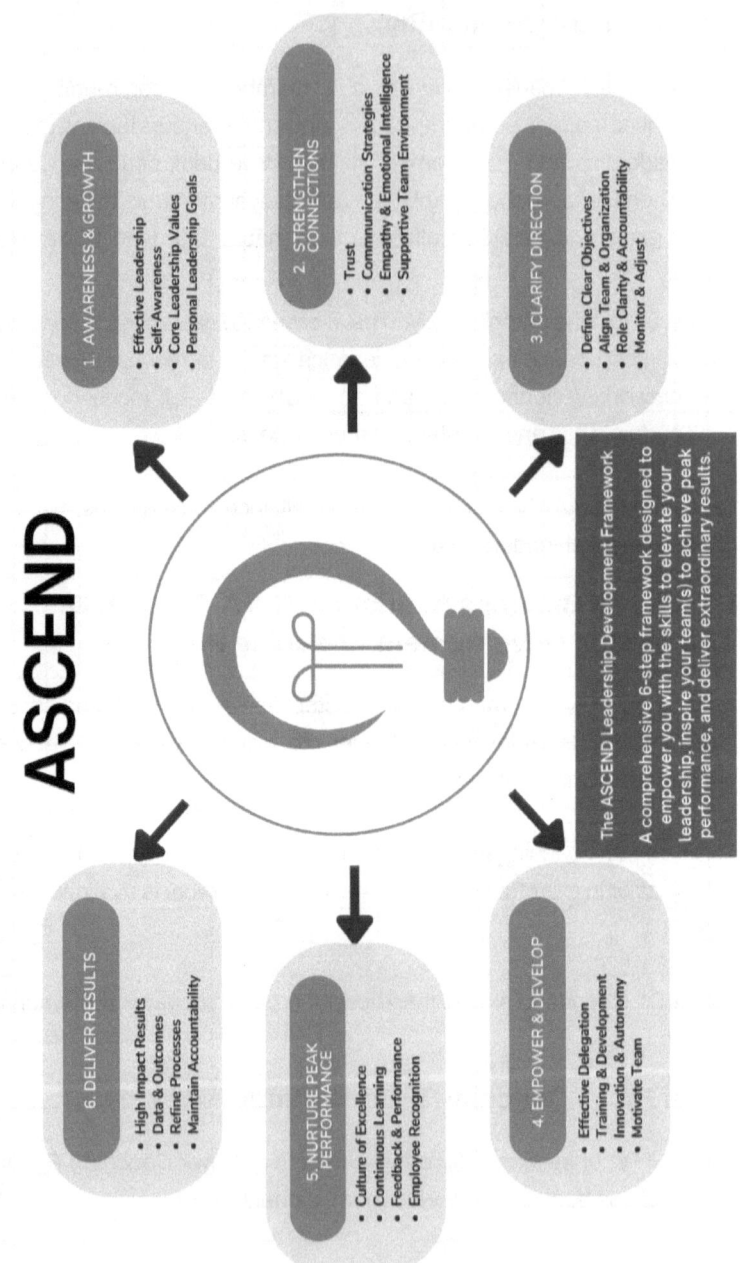

ASCEND

1. AWARENESS & GROWTH
- Effective Leadership
- Self-Awareness
- Core Leadership Values
- Personal Leadership Goals

2. STRENGTHEN CONNECTIONS
- Trust
- Communication Strategies
- Empathy & Emotional Intelligence
- Supportive Team Environment

3. CLARIFY DIRECTION
- Define Clear Objectives
- Align Team & Organization
- Role Clarity & Accountability
- Monitor & Adjust

4. EMPOWER & DEVELOP
- Effective Delegation
- Training & Development
- Innovation & Autonomy
- Motivate Team

5. NURTURE PEAK PERFORMANCE
- Culture of Excellence
- Continuous Learning
- Feedback & Performance
- Employee Recognition

6. DELIVER RESULTS
- High Impact Results
- Data & Outcomes
- Refine Processes
- Maintain Accountability

The ASCEND Leadership Development Framework

A comprehensive 6-step framework designed to empower you with the skills to elevate your leadership, inspire your team(s) to achieve peak performance, and deliver extraordinary results.

REFERENCES

CHAPTER 1

Argyris, C., & Schön, D. A. (1978). *Organizational learning: A theory of action perspective*. Addison-Wesley.

Blanchard, K. (2007). *Leading at a higher level: Blanchard on leadership and creating high-performing organizations*. FT Press.

Blanchard, K., Zigarmi, P., & Zigarmi, D. (1985). *Leadership and the one minute manager: Increasing effectiveness through situational leadership*. William Morrow.

Collins, J. (2001). *Good to great: Why some companies make the leap... and others don't*. HarperBusiness.

Covey, S. R. (1989). *The 7 habits of highly effective people: Powerful lessons in personal change*. Free Press.

Davenport, T. H., & Kirby, J. (2015). *Beyond automation: Strategies for remaining relevant in an era of AI-driven disruption. Harvard Business Review*.

Dweck, C. (2006). *Mindset: The new psychology of success*. Random House.

Goleman, D. (1995). *Emotional intelligence: Why it can matter more than IQ*. Bantam Books.

Goleman, D. (1998). *What makes a leader?* Harvard Business Review.

Greenleaf, R. K. (1977). *Servant leadership: A journey into the nature of legitimate power and greatness*. Paulist Press.

Heifetz, R., & Linsky, M. (2002). *Leadership on the line: Staying alive through the dangers of leading*. Harvard Business Review Press.

Kotter, J. P. (2012). *Leading change*. Harvard Business Review Press.

Lencioni, P. (2002). *The five dysfunctions of a team: A leadership fable*. Jossey-Bass.

Northouse, P. G. (2018). *Leadership: Theory and practice* (8th ed.). SAGE.

Sinek, S. (2009). *Start with why: How great leaders inspire everyone to take action*. Portfolio.

Sinek, S. (2014). *Leaders eat last: Why some teams pull together and others don't.* Portfolio.

CHAPTER 2

Bradberry, T., & Greaves, J. (2009). *Emotional intelligence 2.0.* TalentSmart.

Buckingham, M., & Clifton, D. O. (2001). *Now, discover your strengths.* Free Press.

Goleman, D. (1995). *Emotional intelligence: Why it can matter more than IQ.* Bantam Books.

Rath, T. (2007). *StrengthsFinder 2.0.* Gallup Press.

CHAPTER 3

Covey, S. R. (1989). *The 7 habits of highly effective people: Powerful lessons in personal change.* Free Press.

Dweck, C. (2006). *Mindset: The new psychology of success.* Random House.

Goleman, D. (1995). *Emotional intelligence: Why it can matter more than IQ.* Bantam Books.

Kouzes, J. M., & Posner, B. Z. (2017). *The leadership challenge: How to make extraordinary things happen in organizations.* Wiley.

Rath, T., & Conchie, B. (2008). *Strengths-based leadership: Great leaders, teams, and why people follow.* Gallup Press.

CHAPTER 4

Brown, B. (2018). *Dare to lead: Brave work. Tough conversations. Whole hearts.* Random House.

Covey, S. M. R. (2006). *The speed of trust: The one thing that changes everything.* Free Press.

Edmondson, A. C. (2019). *The fearless organization: Creating psychological safety in the workplace for learning, innovation, and growth.* Wiley.

Kouzes, J. M., & Posner, B. Z. (2017). *The leadership challenge (6th ed.).* Wiley.

Lencioni, P. (2002). *The five dysfunctions of a team: A leadership fable.* Jossey-Bass.

CHAPTER 5

Covey, S. M. R. (2006). *The speed of trust: The one thing that changes everything.* Free Press.

Gallo, A. (2020). *The leader's guide to effective communication.* Harvard Business Review.

Scudder, T., & Canaday, S. (2019). *Communicate like a leader: Connecting strategically to coach, inspire, and get things done.* Wiley.

Watzlawick, P., Bavelas, J. B., & Jackson, D. D. (2011). *Pragmatics of human communication: A study of interactional patterns, pathologies, and paradoxes.* W. W. Norton.

CHAPTER 6

Brown, B. (2018). *Dare to lead: Brave work. Tough conversations. Whole hearts.* Random House.

Covey, S. M. R. (2006). *The speed of trust: The one thing that changes everything.* Free Press.

Edmondson, A. C. (2018). *The fearless organization: Creating psychological safety in the workplace for learning, innovation, and growth.* Wiley.

Shore, L. M., et al. (2011). *Inclusion and diversity in work groups: A review and model for future research. Journal of Management, 37*(4), 1262–1289.

Chapter 7

Doerr, J. (2018). *Measure what matters: OKRs: The simple idea that drives 10x growth*. Portfolio/Penguin.

Drucker, P. F. (1954). *The practice of management*. Harper & Row.

Kaplan, R. S., & Norton, D. P. (1996). *The balanced scorecard: Translating strategy into action*. Harvard Business Review Press.

Locke, E. A., & Latham, G. P. (2002). *Building a practically useful theory of goal setting and task motivation: A 35-year odyssey. American Psychologist, 57*(9), 705–717.

Chapter 8

Buckingham, M., & Goodall, A. (2019). *Nine lies about work: A freethinking leader's guide to the real world*. Harvard Business Review Press.

Duhigg, C. (2016). *Smarter faster better: The secrets of being productive in life and business*. Random House.

Edmondson, A. C. (2019). *The fearless organization: Creating psychological safety in the workplace for learning, innovation, and growth*. Wiley.

Chapter 9

Goleman, D. (1995). *Emotional intelligence: Why it can matter more than IQ*. Bantam Books.

Kouzes, J. M., & Posner, B. Z. (2017). *The leadership challenge: How to make extraordinary things happen in organizations* (6th ed.). Wiley.

Chapter 10

ASTD. (2010). *The ASTD handbook of measuring and evaluating training*. American Society for Training & Development.

Bersin, J. (2014). *The learning organization: A new era of corporate learning and development.* Bersin by Deloitte.

Center for Creative Leadership. (2019). *Leadership development factbook.* https://www.ccl.org

Charan, R., Drotter, S., & Noel, J. (2011). *The leadership pipeline: How to build the leadership powered company* (2nd ed.). Jossey-Bass.

Garvin, D. A., Edmondson, A. C., & Gino, F. (2008). Is yours a learning organization? *Harvard Business Review*, 86(3), 109–116.

Gilley, J. W., & Maycunich, A. (2000). *Beyond the learning organization: Creating a culture of continuous growth and development through state-of-the-art human resource practices.* Perseus Publishing.

Kirkpatrick, D. L., & Kirkpatrick, J. D. (2006). *Evaluating training programs: The four levels* (3rd ed.). Berrett-Koehler.

Lawler, E. E., & Worley, C. G. (2006). *Built to change: How to achieve sustained organizational effectiveness.* Jossey-Bass.

Senge, P. M. (2006). *The fifth discipline: The art & practice of the learning organization* (Rev. ed.). Doubleday.

Ulrich, D., Brockbank, W., Johnson, D., Sandholtz, K., & Younger, J. (2008). *HR competencies: Mastery at the intersection of people and business.* Society for Human Resource Management.

CHAPTER 11

Grote, D. (2020). *How to be good at performance appraisals: Simple, effective, done right.* Harvard Business Review Press.

Gallo, A. (2016). *Giving effective feedback.* Harvard Business Review. https://hbr.org/2016/12/giving-effective-feedback

Adler, S., & Fagley, N. (2005). *Appreciation: Enhancing an Interpersonal Relationship?.* Journal of Personality and Social Psychology, 89(3), 375–386. https://doi.org/10.1037/0022-3514.89.3.375

Kouzes, J. M., & Posner, B. Z. (2017). *The leadership challenge: How to make extraordinary things happen in organizations.* John Wiley & Sons.

Maylett, T. M., & Wride, M. (2017). *The employee experience: How to attract talent, retain top performers, and drive results.* Wiley.

Saks, A. M., & Gruman, J. A. (2014). *Performance management and employee engagement.* Human Resource Management Review, 23(1), 11-19.

Chapter 12

Brynjolfsson, E., & McAfee, A. (2014). *The second machine age: Work, progress, and prosperity in a time of brilliant technologies.* W. W. Norton.

Davenport, T. H., & Bean, R. (2018). *Big data and AI executive survey.* MIT Sloan Management Review.

Marr, B. (2020). *The future of work: How artificial intelligence and automation will transform jobs and industries.* St. Martin's Press.

Chapter 13

Covey, S. R. (1989). *The 7 habits of highly effective people: Powerful lessons in personal change.* Free Press.

Kotter, J. P. (1996). *Leading change.* Harvard Business Review Press.

Sinek, S. (2009). *Start with why: How great leaders inspire everyone to take action.* Penguin.